teach yourself...

Assembler

MARK GOODWIN

MIS:
PRESS

W9-BES-102

© 1991 by Management Information Source, Inc.
P.O. Box 5277
Portland, Oregon 97208-5277

All rights reserved. Reproduction or use of editorial or pictorial content in any
manner is prohibited without express permission. No patent liability is assumed
with respect to the use of the information contained herein. While every precaution
has been taken in the preparation of this book, the publisher assumes no responsibil-
ity for errors or omissions. Neither is any liability assumed for damages resulting
from the use of the information contained herein.

First Printing
ISBN 1-55828-063-4

Printed in the United States of America

TRADEMARKS

IBM is a trademark of IBM Corporation
Microsoft, MS, and MS-DOS are trademarks of Microsoft Corporation
Turbo Assembler is a trademark of Borland International, Inc.

DEDICATION

To my wonderful family:

Denise — The greatest wife and mother there is. I love you more and more every day.

Ryan and Matthew — The two special boys in my life. Nobody could ask for two finer sons.

Crystal — The newest addition to our family. You're a dream come true and I hope the rest of your life is as happy as these first three months have been for you.

Contents

Contents

Contents

Contents

Contents

Introduction

In the early days of computers, there was only one method for programming a computer — machine language programming. The computer pioneers quickly learned that machine language programming was not very practical and so they devised a programming language that represented machine language instructions with symbolic names. They called the symbolic programming language **assembly language programming**. Although assembly language programming was definitely a step in the right direction, computer programmers developed high-level languages like Fortran and COBOL to make life even easier.

Modern computer programmers have a wide range of languages at their disposal. Many programmers prefer C; however, a lot of other languages are widely used, including assembly language. Although it is rare today to see an application program written entirely in assembly language, some devoted assembly language programmers won't give up their language of choice. More often than not, programmers use assembly language combined with a high-level language to speed up certain time-dependent routines. Consequently, this book is written with that in mind. It assumes that you are intimately familiar with a high-level language such as C and want to learn how to use assembly language to enhance your high-level language programs.

While there are excellent optimizing compilers available, there are a number of routines that require the speed that can only be achieved using carefully crafted assembly language code. Additionally, intimate knowledge of the computer helps you to write very efficient high-level language programs and to understand how the computer actually performs its many tasks.

What This Book Teaches You

This book teaches you how to program in assembly language. It covers all of the basic features of assembly language, including

- the elements of an assembly language program
- 8088 architecture
- data representation
- directives and operators
- the 8088 instruction set
- addressing modes
- string handling in assembly language
- structured programming techniques
- structures and records
- stacks
- procedures
- input and output
- interrupt handling
- conditional assembly
- equates and macros
- assembly language routines to enhance C programs.

What This Book Does Not Teach You

This book is not intended to teach you every little detail about assembly language programming. Those details should come from the reference manuals that were packaged with your assembler. Additionally, this book is not intended to teach you a lot of fancy algorithms. If you are an experienced programmer, you may already know a lot about getting a computer program to do what you want.

This book contains numerous program fragments, instead of a lot of complete program samples, to teach you assembly language programming a little bit at a time. By the end of the book, you will be able to put all of these little bits and pieces together to form your own assembly language programs.

What You Need to Use This Book

To use this book, you need an IBM PC or compatible and either Turbo Assembler or the Microsoft Macro Assembler.

Chapter 1

8088 Assembly Language Programming

L earning assembly language programming will help you to write efficient code that enhances your high-level language programs. This chapter helps you to begin your study of assembly language programming by showing you a sample program and by teaching you about

- machine language
- assembly language
- the parts of an 8088 assembly language program
- program assembly
- program execution.

Machine Language

Before you begin your study of assembly language programming, you must understand machine language programming. As its name implies, machine language programming is performed in the language of the computer itself. A digital computer, such as a PC or compatible, only understands two different states: off and on. These two digital states are more commonly represented by the binary digits 0 and 1, respectively. Furthermore, a **binary digit** is traditionally referred to as a **bit**. A statement in a machine language program is comprised of a string of these bits. These bit strings are referred to as **bit patterns**. The following example presents a machine language bit pattern:

```
101110000000010100000000
```

These machine language bit patterns represent instructions, data, and locations of instructions and data. The first eight bits of the previous bit pattern are an 8088 machine language instruction. The last 16 bits of the previous bit pattern represent a data value. The following example illustrates how the computer views the previous bit pattern:

```
10111000          0000010100000000
move ax                  3
```

As the previous example illustrates, the first eight bits of the bit pattern tell the computer to move the 16-bit number that follows the instruction into a storage location called AX. These storage locations are called **registers**. In the case of the above instruction, the machine language instruction tells the CPU to store a value of 3 in its **AX** register.

Although machine language is fascinating, it can be very hard to understand. After all, a machine language program can be constructed from an almost limitless variety of bit patterns. Remembering what bit pattern performs what function is too much for even the best programmer to remember. To present these machine language instructions in a much more accessible form, early programmers devised a method for representing machine language instructions using a language called assembly language.

Assembly Language

In assembly language, machine language instructions are given special names called **mnemonics**. Additionally, data can be represented by using a numeric value (such as,

5, 16, 0bfh, 33, 555, or 1) or a symbolic name (such as, MAX, count, line, or RESULT). The following example shows how the previous machine language bit pattern could be represented by an assembly language statement:

```
mov      ax,3
```

To say the least, the previous assembly language statement is far easier to remember than its corresponding machine language bit pattern. Unfortunately, the computer is unable to recognize what the previous assembly language statement means. To translate the previous statement into a form that the computer can understand, you must use an assembler. The assembler simply translates assembly language program statements into equivalent machine language bit patterns.

The Parts of the Program

An 8088 assembly language program is comprised of four basic parts:

- code segments
- data segments
- labels
- comments.

Code Segments

Essentially, the code segments are the portions of the program that contain instructions. These instructions can perform a wide variety of tasks, such as moving data, controlling program flow, or performing arithmetic functions. Each assembly language instruction is constructed from two basic parts: the operation and the operands. The following example illustrates how the **mov ax,3** instruction is constructed:

```
Operation      Operands

mov            ax,3
```

As the previous example demonstrates, the mov mnemonic tells the CPU to move a piece of data. The operands, **ax,3**, tell the CPU that the value to be moved is a 3 and it is to be moved into the **AX** register. While all assembly language instructions require an operation, not all require operands. For example, the following statement tells the 8088 CPU to ignore all maskable interrupts:

```
cli
```

Data Segments

Although code segments are essential, almost all 8088 assembly language programs require at least one data segment. A data segment is the portion of an assembly language program where data is stored. For example, a program that needs three 16-bit variables (**a**, **b**, **c**) requires the following data statements:

```
a          dw      3
b          dw      4
c          dw      ?
```

The three **dw**s in the above statements are **assembler directives**, that direct the assembler to define three words. In the case of the 8088, a word is 16 bits long. Therefore, the above three statements define the three desired 16-bit variables. Although it's obvious that a value of **3** is stored in the 16-bit location **a** and a value of **4** is stored in the 16-bit location **b**, it is not obvious what is stored in 16-bit location **c**. Essentially, the **?** in the previous data statement tells the assembler that the 16-bit location **c** is undefined. Therefore, do not assume that **c** is set to any particular value.

Labels

The symbolic names **a**, **b**, and **c** in the above example data statements are good examples of assembly language labels. In addition to being used as a variable names, an assembly language label can also be used as a name, such as a segment name or a procedure name. Valid 8088 assembly language labels can be composed of digits, letters, and the characters **?**, **.**, **@**, **_**, and **$**. Additionally, a name cannot start with a digit and a period can only be used as a label's first character. Labels can be any length, but only the first 31 characters are significant. Unless a label is used in conjunction with an assembler directive, it must be immediately followed by a **:** (colon).

Comments

The fourth component of an assembly language program is the comment. As its name implies, the comment describes what the program does and has no actual effect on the operation of the program. Although comments may not seem essential, they are an important part of any program. Usually you will either need to debug or modify a program at some future date. Use comments judiciously to reduce the amount of time you will need to relearn how the program performs its intended functions. You create comments in an 8088 assembly language program by simply starting them with a ; (semicolon). The following examples show some assembly language comments:

```
        mov     ax,3     ;AX is set to 3
    ; The previous instruction sets register AX to 3
```

A Sample Assembly Language Program

The following example shows a fairly short 8088 assembly language program. Although this program is relatively simple, it points out a number of key elements that make up an assembly language program. First, examine the following program. Then examine the same program as it is explained one line at a time.

```
;
; first.asm - A first assembly language program
;
;
; Code segment
;
_TEXT        segment word public 'CODE'
             assume  cs:_TEXT,ds:_DATA,ss:_STACK
;
; Add two 16 bit values
;
```

continued...

...from previous page

```
addem          proc      far                  ;Entry point from DOS
               mov       ax,_DATA             ;Point the data segment
               mov       ds,ax                ; register to the data
                                              ; segment
               mov       ax,a                 ;AX = a
               add       ax,b                 ;AX = a + b
               mov       c,ax                 ;c = a + b
               mov       ax,4c00h             ;AX = No error return
                                              ; code
               int       21h                  ;Return to DOS
addem          endp
_TEXT          ends
;
; Data segment
;
_DATA          segment word public 'DATA'
a              dw        3
b              dw        4
c              dw        ?
_DATA          ends
;
; Stack segment
;
_STACK         segment para stack 'STACK'
               db        128 dup (?)
_STACK         ends
               end       addem               ;Defines the entry point
```

Line-by-Line Program Explanation

```
;
; first.asm - A first assembly language program
;
```

is a comment that shows the program name, **first.asm**, and gives a brief explanation about the program's purpose.

```
;
; Code segment
;
```

is a comment explaining that a code segment follows.

```
_TEXT          segment word public 'CODE'
```

declares the start of a **CODE** segment and assigns the label **_TEXT** to the segment.

```
        assume   cs:_TEXT,ds:_DATA,ss:_STACK
```

assume is an assembler directive that tells the assembler what segments the 8088 segment registers are pointing to. In this case, the assembler is to "assume" that the 8088 code segment register **CS** is pointing to the **_TEXT** segment, the 8088 data segment register **DS** is pointing to the **_DATA** segment, and the 8088 stack segment register **SS** is pointing to the **_STACK** segment. Note that all of these are assumption on the part of the assembler. The segment registers may or may not be actually pointing to the indicated segments.

```
        ;
        ; Add two 16-bit values
        ;
```

is a comment that explains the purpose of the procedure that follows.

```
        addem        proc      far              ;Entry point from DOS
```

declares the start of a procedure called **addem**. Furthermore, the procedure is a **far** call.

```
                mov      ax,_DATA       ;Point the data segment
```

moves the segment address of the **_DATA** segment into register **AX**.

```
                mov      ds,ax          ;register to the data
                                        ;segment
```

sets the 8088 data segment register to point to the **_DATA** segment. Since **first.asm** is a DOS EXE program, DOS automatically sets the 8088 code segment register to point to the **_TEXT** segment and the 8088 stack segment register to the **_STACK** segment upon entry to the program. However, the appropriate value for the 8088 data segment register must be manually set by the program.

```
        mov      ax,a              ;AX = a
```

moves the value stored in memory at the location with the symbolic name **a** into register **AX**.

```
        add      ax,b              ;AX = a + b
```

adds the value stored in memory at the location with the symbolic name **b** with the value already residing in register **AX**. Note that the result of the addition operation will be left in register **AX**.

```
        mov      c,ax              ;c = a + b
```

saves the result of the addition operation in the memory location indicated by the symbolic name **c**.

```
        mov      ax,4c00h          ;AX = No error return code
        int      21h               ;Return to DOS
```

returns program control back to MS-DOS.

```
        addem        endp
```

tells the assembler that the procedure **addem** has **end**ed.

```
    _TEXT        ends
```

tells the assembler that the segment **_TEXT** has **end**ed.

```
        ;

        ;  Data segment

        ;
```

is a comment explaining that a data segment is about to follow.

```
    _DATA           segment word public 'DATA'
```

declares the start of a **DATA** segment and assigns the label **_DATA** to the segment.

```
    a               dw          3
```

directs the assembler to make room for a 16-bit word with an initial value of 3 and a symbolic name of **a**.

```
    b               dw          4
```

directs the assembler to make room for a 16-bit word with an initial value of 4 and a symbolic name of **b**.

```
    c               dw          ?
```

directs the assembler to make room for a 16-bit word that has no initial value and a symbolic name of **c**.

```
    _DATA           ends
```

tells the assembler that the segment **_DATA** has **end**ed.

```
;
; Stack segment
;
```

is a comment explaining that a stack segment follows.

```
_STACK        segment para stack 'STACK'
```

declares a **STACK** segment and assigns the label **_STACK** to the segment. Essentially, a stack segment is a very special type of data segment. It is generally used to hold transient data for both the CPU and the program.

```
db      128 dup (?)
```

directs the assembler to leave room for **128** bytes of unknown value.

```
_STACK        ends
```

tells the assembler that the **_STACK** segment has **end**ed.

```
end     addem           ;Defines the entry point
```

tells the assembler that it has reached the end of the program. It also tells the assembler that the code immediately following the **addem** label is the point where MS-DOS will enter the program.

Assembling Your First Program

Although the above program example provides insight into the structure of an 8088 assembly language program, it does not show how you actually create a program. The first step in creating an assembly language program is to use a text editor to enter the **source code** of the program. The source code is simply a text file for the program. With a copy of the source code for the previous program available on disk, you can assemble it with the Microsoft Macro Assembler (MASM) using the following command line:

```
masm first.asm;
```

If you are using the Turbo Assembler (TASM) to assemble the program, enter the following command line:

```
tasm first.asm;
```

If you correctly entered the source code for **first.asm**, the assembler produced an **object module** with the name **first.obj**. This object module is the translation of the assembly language source code into machine language.

The program requires one final step before it can actually be run. This final phase in the assembly language program creation cycle is called linking. This process of linking the program turns the assembler-generated object module into an executable file called **first.exe**. To create **first.exe** with the Microsoft Linker, you can use the following command line:

```
link first;
```

Additionally, you can link **first.exe** with Turbo Linker by using the following command line:

```
tlink first;
```

Running the Program

Now that you have created a DOS-executable version of the program, you can execute it with the following DOS command:

```
first
```

If you tried executing **first**, you are now probably wondering what went wrong. After entering the proper command line, the MS-DOS system prompt is almost immediately

displayed. Although this may seem like an incorrect result, the program really did perform its intended function. You can verify this by using **debug** to look at the inner
workings of the program. To check out **first** with **debug**, enter the following DOS
command:

```
debug first.exe
```

You will be greeted with the **debug** prompt. At this prompt, enter a **u**. The **u** command
instructs debug to **u**nassemble (or more properly: disassemble) the following 20 bytes.
The following listing is what **debug** produces:

```
2131:0000  B83221        MOV      AX,2132
2131:0003  8ED8          MOV      DS,AX

2131:0005  A10400        MOV      AX,[0004]

2131:0008  03060600      ADD      AX,[0006]

2131:000C  A30800        MOV      [0008],AX

2131:000F  B8004C        MOV      AX,4C00

2131:0012  CD21          INT      21

2131:0014  0300          ADD      AX,[BX+SI]

2131:0016  0400          ADD      AL,00

2131:0018  0000          ADD      [BX+SI],AL

2131:001A  1B894         SBB      CX,[BX+DI+F646]

2131:001E  A1D84         MOV      AX,[43D8]
```

If you compare the first seven lines of this disassembled listing with the seven lines of
code in the code segment of **first.asm**, you will see that the instructions and operands
are almost identical. The only difference is that the original source code used symbolic
names like **_STACK**, **a**, **b**, and **c**, while the disassembled listing used their actual
memory locations.

You can use the debug **t** command to view how the program actually performs its intended function. The debug **t** command tells debug to execute the next machine language instruction, display the resulting contents of the 8088's registers, and then display a disassembled version of the next machine language instruction. Enter **t** to display the following results:

```
-t
AX=2132  BX=0000  CX=001A  DX=0000  SP=0080  BP=0000  SI=0000  DI=0000
DS=2121  ES=2121  SS=2133  CS=2131  IP=0003    NV UP EI PL NZ NA PO NC
2131:0003 8ED8          MOV     DS,AX
```

Notice how **AX** now holds the segment address (2132H) for the **_DATA** segment. (Note that the actual segment address varies depending on your version of DOS and whether or not any TSRs are loaded into memory.) Continue by executing the **MOV DS,AX** instruction:

```
-t
AX=2132  BX=0000  CX=001A  DX=0000  SP=0080  BP=0000  SI=0000  DI=0000
DS=2132  ES=2121  SS=2133  CS=2131  IP=0005    NV UP EI PL NZ NA PO NC
2131:0005 A10400         MOV     AX,[0004]
DS:0004=0003
```

The **DS** register now holds the same value as register **AX**. Execute the **MOV AX,[0004]** instruction:

```
-t
AX=0003  BX=0000  CX=001A  DX=0000  SP=0080  BP=0000  SI=0000  DI=0000
DS=2132  ES=2121  SS=2133  CS=2131  IP=0008    NV UP EI PL NZ NA PO NC
2131:0008 03060600       ADD     AX,[0006]
DS:0006=0004
```

AX now holds the value of **a**. Execute the **ADD AX,[0006]** instruction:

```
-t
AX=0007     BX=0000  CX=001A  DX=0000  SP=0080  BP=0000  SI=0000  DI=0000
DS=2132     ES=2121  SS=2133  CS=2131  IP=000C   NV UP EI PL NZ NA PO NC
2131:000C A30800          MOV      [0008],AX
DS:0008=0000
```

AX is now equal to the sum of **a** plus **b**. Execute the **MOV [0008],AX** instruction:

```
-t
AX=0007  BX=0000  CX=001A  DX=0000  SP=0080  BP=0000  SI=0000  DI=0000
DS=2132  ES=2121  SS=2133  CS=2131  IP=000F   NV UP EI PL NZ NA PO NC
2131:000F B8004C     MOV      AX,4C00
```

There. The location with the symbolic name **c** is now equal the sum of **a** plus **b**. But how can you prove it? It's really quite simple. The **debug d** command enables you to display the contents of any memory location. Look at location 0008 (as you can see, that's the location with the name **c** because of the previous instruction) with the following debug command:

```
-d 8
2132:0000                  07 00 1B 89 46 F6 A1 D8      ....F...
2132:0010 43 8B 16 DA 43 89 46 EA-89 56 EC EB 2A 90 A1 D6   C...C.F..V..*...
2132:0020 16 0B 06 D8 16 74 1D C4-5E EE 26 8A 47 16 24 07   .....t..^.&.G.$.
2132:0030 3C 01 75 10 A1 4E 1F 89-46 F6 A1 D6 16 8B 16 D8   <.u..N..F.......
2132:0040 16 EB D2 90 89 7E F6 8D-45 01 89 46 E6 E9 38 03   .....~..E..F..8.
2132:0050 C4 5E EE 26 8A 5F 0E 2A-FF D1 E3 D1 E3 FF B7 7C   .^.&._.*.......|
2132:0060 20 FF B7 7A 20 2B C0 50-E8 85 22 52 50 E8 30 2D   ..z +.P.."RP.0-
2132:0070 40 50 8A 5E FE 2A FF D1-E3 D1 E3 FF B7 7C 20 FF   @P.^.*.......| .
2132:0080 B7 7A 20 2B C0 50 07 00                           .z +.P..
```

As you can see from this listing, **c** has been set to the value of **a** plus **b**. Since you have been using debug to execute the program, you can return to DOS by using the **debug q** (quit) command.

```
-q
```

Summary

In this chapter, you learned the difference between machine language and assembly language programming and studied the four basic elements of an assembly language program. Additionally, you learned how to create, assemble, link, and execute an actual assembly language program. Finally, you examined the resulting program's inner workings with **debug**.

Chapter 2

8088 Architecture

U nderstanding how a computer manipulates data will help you to better understand the methodologies behind 8088 assembly language programming. This chapter teaches you about

- storage elements
- the 8088 register set
- computer memory
- input/output devices.

Storage Elements

The first step in understanding how a computer is constructed (its **architecture**) is to learn the basic storage elements that represent machine language instructions and data values. The 8088 assembly language features seven basic storage element types: **bits**, **nibbles**, **bytes**, **words**, **doublewords**, **quadwords**, and **tenbytes**. Look at these seven basic storage element types one at a time.

Bits

A digital computer represents data as a string of binary digits. These binary digits are called bits and each individual digit can be equal to either 0 or 1. Figure 2-1 illustrates a bit that is equal to 1.

$$\boxed{1}$$

Figure 2-1. A Bit.

Although bits are the most basic of the 8088 storage elements, they are not really useful by themselves. After all, you cannot represent a wide variety of data with a storage element that has only two different values. Accordingly, the 8088 has a number of other storage elements that are much better suited for representing a diverse assortment of data.

Nibbles

The next largest storage element type is the nibble. A nibble is a sequence of four individual bits. By convention, the bits in a nibble are numbered from right to left, where the rightmost bit (least significant bit) is bit 0 and the leftmost bit (most significant bit) is bit 3. Figure 2-2 illustrates a sequence of four bits that make up a nibble.

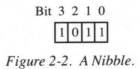

Bit 3 2 1 0

Figure 2-2. A Nibble.

Bytes

The next size up from a nibble is a byte. A byte is constructed from a sequence of eight bits. The bits in a byte are numbered from right to left like the bits of a nibble. Figure 2-3 illustrates a sequence of eight bits that make up a byte.

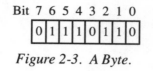

Figure 2-3. A Byte.

Words

The next size up from a byte is a word. A word is constructed from a sequence of 16 individual bits. Like nibbles and bytes, the bits in a word are numbered from right to left. Note that the least significant byte (bits 0 to 7) is stored in memory before the most significant byte (bits 8 to 15). Figure 2-4 illustrates a word stored in memory as sequence of two bytes.

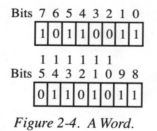

Figure 2-4. A Word.

Doublewords

The next step up from a word is the doubleword. The doubleword is constructed from a sequence of 32 bits. The bits of a doubleword are numbered from right to left. Additionally, the least significant byte (bits 0 to 7) is stored in memory first, the next most significant byte (bits 8 to 15) is stored next, the next most significant byte (bits 16 to 23) follows, and finally the most significant byte (bits 24 to 31) is stored in memory last. Figure 2-5 illustrates a doubleword stored as a series of four bytes.

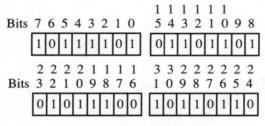

Figure 2-5. A Doubleword.

Quadwords

The next step up from a doubleword is a quadword. The quadword is constructed from a sequence of 64 bits. As with the preceding storage types, the bits of a quadword are numbered from right to left and its bytes are stored with the least significant byte first and the most significant byte last. Figure 2-6 illustrates a quadword stored as a series of eight bytes.

```
                                        1 1 1 1 1 1 1 1
       Bits  7 6 5 4 3 2 1 0            5 4 3 2 1 0 9 8
            +-+-+-+-+-+-+-+-+          +-+-+-+-+-+-+-+-+
            |1|0|1|1|0|1|0|1|          |1|0|1|0|0|1|0|1|
            +-+-+-+-+-+-+-+-+          +-+-+-+-+-+-+-+-+

             2 2 2 2 1 1 1 1            3 3 2 2 2 2 2 2
       Bits  3 2 1 0 9 8 7 6            1 0 9 8 7 6 5 4
            +-+-+-+-+-+-+-+-+          +-+-+-+-+-+-+-+-+
            |1|1|1|1|0|0|0|0|          |0|0|0|1|1|1|1|1|
            +-+-+-+-+-+-+-+-+          +-+-+-+-+-+-+-+-+

             3 3 3 3 3 3 3 3            4 4 4 4 4 4 4 4
       Bits  9 8 7 6 5 4 3 2            7 6 5 4 3 2 1 0
            +-+-+-+-+-+-+-+-+          +-+-+-+-+-+-+-+-+
            |1|0|1|1|0|1|0|1|          |1|0|1|0|0|1|0|1|
            +-+-+-+-+-+-+-+-+          +-+-+-+-+-+-+-+-+

             5 5 5 5 5 5 4 4            6 6 6 6 5 5 5 5
       Bits  5 4 3 2 1 0 9 8            3 2 1 0 9 8 7 6
            +-+-+-+-+-+-+-+-+          +-+-+-+-+-+-+-+-+
            |1|1|1|1|0|0|0|0|          |0|0|0|0|1|1|1|1|
            +-+-+-+-+-+-+-+-+          +-+-+-+-+-+-+-+-+
```

Figure 2-6. A Quadword.

Tenbytes

The largest storage unit in the 8088 is the tenbyte. The tenbyte is a sequence of 10 bytes or 80 bits. As with the preceding storage types, the bits in a tenbyte are numbered from right to left and its bytes are stored in memory with the least significant byte first and the most significant byte last. Figure 2-7 illustrates a tenbyte that is stored as a series of 10 bytes.

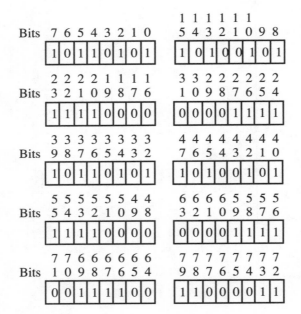

Figure 2-7. A Tenbyte.

The 8088 Register Set

The 8088 microprocessor has a number of special memory locations called registers. Figure 2-8 illustrates the 8088 register set. As this illustration shows, the 8088 has a very diverse set of registers.

General Purpose Registers

```
        15                    0
AX    │ AH    │ AL   │
BX    │ BH    │ BL   │
CX    │ CH    │ CL   │
DX    │ DH    │ DL   │
BP    │              │
SI    │              │
DI    │              │
SP    │              │
```

Segment Registers

```
CS    │              │
DS    │              │
ES    │              │
SS    │              │
```

Other Registers

```
Flags │              │
IP    │              │
```

Figure 2-8. The 8088 Register Set.

27

Examine each of these registers in more detail to see how they are generally used.

Register AX

The **AX** register is the accumulator. It is a 16-bit general purpose register. An 8088 general purpose register stores any 16-bit value, moves data to and from memory, and performs arithmetic and logical operations. Additionally, register **AX** can be accessed as two 8-bit registers. The two 8-bit registers that make up register **AX** are registers **AH** and **AL**. Register **AH** references the most significant byte in **AX**. Register **AL** references the least significant byte in **AX**. Register **AX** is generally used to hold temporary data. Many of the 8088 instructions (such as, addition or subtraction) perform their functions much faster if you use register **AX**.

Register BX

The **BX** register is a base register. It is a 16-bit general purpose register that can be accessed as two 8-bit registers. The two 8-bit registers that make up register **BX** are registers **BH** and **BL**. Register **BH** references most significant byte in **BX**. Register **BL** references the least significant byte in **BX**. Register **BX** is primarily used as a pointer; however, it can also be used for data storage.

Register CX

The **CX** register a counter. It is a 16-bit general purpose register that can be accessed as two 8-bit registers. The two 8-bit registers that make up register **CX** are registers **CH** and **CL**. Register **CH** references the most significant byte in **CX**. Register **CL** references the least significant byte in **CX**. Register **CX** is primarily used to hold a count for instructions that either loop or repeat. Register **CX** can also be used for data storage.

Register DX

The **DX** register is a data register. It is a 16-bit general purpose register that can be accessed as two 8-bit registers. The two 8-bit registers that make up register **DX** are registers **DH** and **DL**. Register **DH** references the most significant byte in **DX.** Register **DL** references the least significant byte in **DX**. Register **DX** is often used for doubleword arithmetic operations and to hold the port number during port input/output operations. Register **DX** is also used for temporary data storage.

Register BP

The **BP** register is the base pointer. It is a 16-bit general purpose register and is generally used to point to high-level language stack frames. However, register **BP** can be used for temporary data storage. The stack segment (register **SS**) is assumed to be the segment register to which **BP** points.

Register SI

The **SI** register is the source index register. It is a 16-bit general purpose register and is primarily used as a pointer. Register **SI** is the source pointer during string operations. Besides its function as a pointer, register **SI** can be used for temporary data storage.

Register DI

The **DI** register is the destination index register. It is a 16-bit general purpose register that is primarily used as a pointer. Register **DI** is the destination pointer during string operations. Besides its function as a pointer, register **DI** can be used for temporary data storage.

Register SP

The **SP** register is the stack pointer. It is a 16-bit general purpose register that points to the current location of the stack in the stack segment (register **SS**).

Register IP

The **IP** register is the instruction pointer. It is a 16-bit register that points to the next instruction to be executed.

Register CS

The **CS** register is the code segment register. It is a 16-bit register that points to the memory segment with the instructions and operands of the assembly language program. To better understand how the code segment register and the other segment registers (**DS**, **ES**, and **SS**) function, examine how the 8088 addresses memory. The 8088 microprocessor can address up to one megabyte of memory.

The 8088 index and pointer registers (**BX**, **BP**, **DI**, **IP**, and **SI**) are all 16-bit registers. A 16-bit register can only point to 65,536 (64K) different memory locations. Consequently, the 8088 uses a segmented architecture to overcome this 64K segment limitation. Essentially, the 8088 joins the index or pointer register with an appropriate segment register to determine the correct memory location. When combining the segment register with the index or pointer register, the 8088 multiplies the value in the segment register by 16 and adds the contents of the index or pointer register to the result. Thus, the 8088 can effectively address a full megabyte of memory (16 * 65536 = 1048576).

Register DS

The **DS** register is the data segment register. It is a 16-bit register that is primarily used to point to the segment with the allocated data in the assembly language program.

Register ES

The **ES** register is the extra segment register. It is a 16-bit register that is used by a number of the 8088 string operations. Additionally, a temporary segment address can be stored in register **ES**.

Register SS

The SS register is the stack segment register. It is a 16-bit register that points to the stack area in the assembly language program. The program and the CPU both use the stack area to hold temporary data values.

The Flags Register

The flags register indicates a result for a number of the 8088 instructions. The flags register is a 16-bit register, where each bit has a special meaning. Figure 2-9 illustrates how the 8088 uses the bits in the flag register.

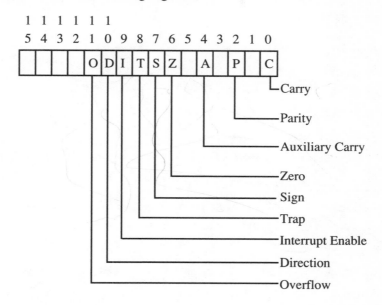

Figure 2-9. The Flags Register.

The carry flag

The carry flag is set (1) by an operation to indicate a carry from or a borrow to.

The parity flag

The parity flag is set (1) if the result of an operation has an even number of bits set to 1.

The auxiliary carry flag

The auxiliary carry flag is set (1) if the low-order four bits of an operation generates a carry from or a borrow to. The auxiliary carry flag is used for binary-coded decimal arithmetic.

The zero flag

The zero flag is set (1) if the result of an operation is 0.

The sign flag

The **sign** flag is set (1) if the result of an operation is negative. Otherwise, the **sign** flag is cleared (0) to indicate a positive result.

The trap flag

Whenever the **trap** flag is set (1), a single-step interrupt is generated after each instruction is executed. By using the **trap** flag, a debugger can single-step through a program.

The interrupt enable flag

If the **interrupt enable** flag is set (1), the 8088 recognizes all maskable interrupts.

The direction flag

If the **direction** flag is set (1), all 8088 string operations work in a downwards direction. Otherwise, a cleared **direction** flag causes the 8088 string operations to work upwards in memory.

The overflow flag

The **overflow** flag is set (1) to indicate that an operation's result was either too large or too small for the destination operand.

Computer Memory

The 8088 microprocessor needs a number of other devices to become a functional system. The most important of these other devices is memory. There are two basic types of computer memory: random access memory (RAM) and read only memory (ROM). Random access memory is any memory that can be both written to and read from. Read only memory is any memory that can be read from but not written to.

Input and Output

Now that you have a computer with a CPU and some memory, you need other devices in order to communicate with the computer. Additionally, you need somewhere to store and retrieve both programs and data. The devices that fill these communication and storage requirements are known as input/output devices. Input/output devices can be broken down into three major classifications: input devices, output devices, and input/output devices.

Input Devices

An input device is any device that can be used to send data to the computer. Examples of input devices include keyboards, mice, trackballs, joysticks, digitizing pads, scanners, and CD-ROM drives. As this list indicates, input devices are mainly used to allow humans to communicate with the computer.

Output Devices

An output device is any device that can be used to get data from the computer. Examples of output devices include video displays, printers, and plotters. Output devices are chiefly used to allow the computer to communicate something to its human operator.

Input/Output Devices

An input/output device is any device that can send data to the computer and get data from the computer. Examples of input/output devices include modems, floppy disk drives, hard disk drives, and optical disk drives. Although such devices as modems allow for communication with another computer, input/output devices are generally used to store and retrieve computer programs and data.

Summary

In this chapter, you learned about the 8088 microprocessor's fundamental storage element types, registers, and segmented architecture. Additionally, you learned about the devices that are required to make a computer a functional device: computer memory, input devices, output devices, and input/output devices.

Chapter **3**

Data Representation

Although the binary numbering system used by computers can represent virtually any number, it is difficult to think in terms of binary numbers. Therefore, you use a variety of numbering systems to simplify how numbers are represented in a computer program. This chapter teaches you about how the 8088 assembly language uses

- binary numbers
- the decimal number system
- the hexadecimal number system
- positive and negative numbers
- Booleans
- binary-coded decimals
- floating point numbers
- characters and strings.

Binary Numbers

Since binary numbers are the language of the digital computer, it is very important that you become well versed in their uses. Although other number systems may be more important to you, it is essential to perform certain tasks using binary numbers. Figure 3-1 illustrates how a byte is used to represent binary numbers.

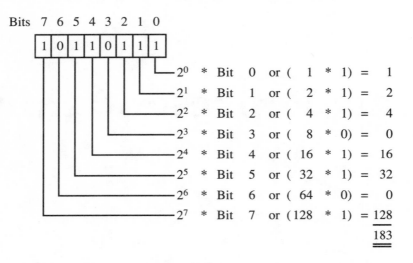

$$
\begin{aligned}
\text{Bits } 7\ 6\ 5\ 4\ 3\ 2\ 1\ 0 \\[4pt]
1\ 0\ 1\ 1\ 0\ 1\ 1\ 1
\end{aligned}
$$

2^0	*	Bit	0	or (	1	*	1)	=	1
2^1	*	Bit	1	or (	2	*	1)	=	2
2^2	*	Bit	2	or (	4	*	1)	=	4
2^3	*	Bit	3	or (	8	*	0)	=	0
2^4	*	Bit	4	or (	16	*	1)	=	16
2^5	*	Bit	5	or (	32	*	1)	=	32
2^6	*	Bit	6	or (	64	*	0)	=	0
2^7	*	Bit	7	or (	128	*	1)	=	128
									183

Figure 3-1. The Binary Number System.

As Figure 3-1 illustrates, each digit in the binary number system is a power of 2 and the power of 2 that each digit represents is directly derived from its bit number.

The Decimal Number System

The decimal number system (or base 10) is the number system we all use in our day-to-day tasks. Essentially, each digit in a decimal number is a power of 10. Figure 3-2 illustrates the wide range of numbers a 5-digit decimal number can represent.

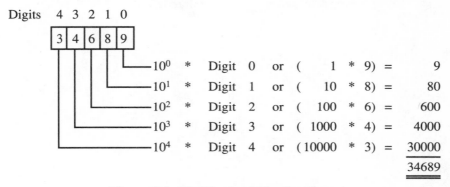

Figure 3-2. The Decimal Number System.

People have an innate ability for understanding decimal numbers, but not binary numbers. Humans have an easy time visualizing base 10. Whether it's just because it's the system our society has adopted or if there is something truly mystical about the decimal number system, decimal numbers are the easiest for computer programmers to work with. Unfortunately, decimal numbers are not always the best way to represent data in an assembly language program.

The Hexadecimal Number System

The hexadecimal number system (or base 16) is perhaps the most widely used number system for representing data in an assembly language program. Since each hexadecimal digit can represent the numbers 0 to 15, each hexadecimal digit can represent one nibble of data. Remember, a nibble of data is a sequence of four bits; therefore, a nibble can hold the values 0000 (0) to 1111 (15).

Being able to represent 16 distinct values with only one digit presents a slight problem. How are the numbers 10 to 15 represented in a hexadecimal number? The hexadecimal number system uses the numeric characters 0, 1, 2, 3, 4, 5, 6, 7, 8, and 9 to represent the values 0 to 9. Additionally, the hexadecimal number system uses the alphabetic characters A, B, C, D, E, and F (or a, b, c, d, e, and f) to represent the values 10 to 15. The following table shows how all 16 hexadecimal values are represented:

Numeric Value	Character
0	0
1	1
2	2
3	3
4	4
5	5
6	6
7	7
8	8
9	9
10	A or a
11	B or b
12	C or c
13	D or d
14	E or e
15	F or f

Since each hexadecimal digit can represent a nibble, the hexadecimal number system is well suited for assembly language programming. Figure 3-3 illustrates how a word of data is represented by a 4-digit hexadecimal number. This figure shows that the hexadecimal number system is much better than the binary number system for representing many of the numbers that you are likely to encounter. Furthermore, the hexadecimal number system is often superior to the decimal number system because it is able to cleanly represent the boundaries for bytes, words, and the like that are found in an assembly language program.

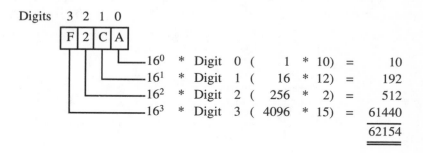

Figure 3-3. The Hexadecimal Number System.

Positive and Negative Numbers

So far, you have only worked with unsigned integer values. An integer is a number that does not have a fractional part. Although a lot of numbers in an assembly language program do not require a sign, many types of data do require signed values. A sign bit is assigned for each piece of data to indicate positive and negative values. Figure 3-4 illustrates how the sign bit is implemented in a byte value. As the figure shows, the sign bit is the most significant bit and is set to 0 to indicate positive numbers and set to 1 to indicate negative numbers.

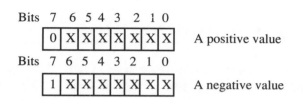

Figure 3-4. Positive and Negative Numbers.

Since the sign requires a bit of its own, a signed byte value can only use seven bits to represent values; therefore, a signed byte value can represent positive numbers in the range of 0 to 127. But how do you represent negative values? A first consideration might be to just simply invert all of positive values bits. This type of bit inversion is called a 1's complement. Unfortunately, doing a simple 1's complement doesn't quite work. Figure 3-5 illustrates the reason why.

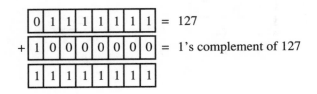

Figure 3-5. Adding 127 and It's 1's complement.

As you can see from this illustration, adding a 127 to a −127, which was figured using a 1's complement, yields a result of all 1s. Obviously, this is the wrong result (127 + −127 = 0). You could, however, get the correct result by simply adding 1 to the result. Figure 3-6 illustrates how 1 can be added to the previous result.

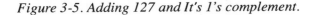

Figure 3-6. Adjusting The 1's Complement Result.

By applying the same principle that is illustrated in Figure 3-6, you can form negative numbers by a method called 2's complement. To convert from a positive number to a negative number, you simply perform a 1's complement on the value and add one. This same method works when converting a negative number to a positive number. Figure 3-7 illustrates how −127 is determined by performing a 2's complement on 127.

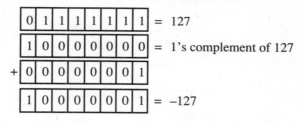

Figure 3-7. Figuring the 2's Complement of 127.

Finally, Figure 3-8 illustrates that the value calculated in Figure 3-7 is indeed −127 by adding it to 127. Since the 2's complement has been used this time to figure the correct value for −127, the proper result of 0 is achieved by the operation.

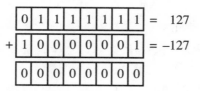

Figure 3-8. Calculating 127 + −127.

Booleans

Boolean values represent the values True and False. These two logical values are represented in a single bit as 1 for True and 0 for False. In storage sizes that are larger than a bit, Booleans are represented by duplicating their appropriate bit values throughout the bits in a storage element. Thus, a byte with a True value would be set to FF_{16} and a byte with a False value would be set to 00_{16}. Figure 3-9 illustrates how True would be represented in a byte value. A word set to True would be equal to $FFFF_{16}$.

1	1	1	1	1	1	1	1

Figure 3-9. A Byte Representation of True.

Note that many high-level languages use either integer or byte values of 1 and 0 to represent the logical values of True and False respectively. If you use the 8088 assembly language Boolean method in an assembly language subroutine that has been written for use with a high-level language, you might have problems. The problems could arise because of the differences between the way Booleans are represented by the high-level language and by assembly language. Consequently, you must be sure that whenever a Boolean value is passed to a high-level language routine, that it is in a form that the high-level language can use.

Binary-Coded Decimals

Many programs, particularly business applications, require decimal point numbers. There are two basic ways to store decimal point numbers: as binary-coded decimals or as floating point numbers. The easiest to understand and the most accurate of these two data types is binary-coded decimals. To encode a number as a binary coded decimal, each of the numbers digits is stored as a nibble. For example if you wanted to store the number 53 as a binary-coded decimal, you would store it as a byte with the value 53^6.

Since the number is stored as 53^{16} and not 53^{10}, you must be careful not to mix binary-coded decimals with other data types. If the example binary-coded decimal was mistakenly used as binary number, the computer would interpret the number as 83^{10} (5 * 16 + 3). To handle binary-coded decimals, the 8088 has a number of special instructions that are intended just for working with them. Although using binary-coded decimals requires a little extra work (such as, keeping track of the decimal point, or using special binary-coded decimal 8088 instructions), it is the best method for storing decimal numbers where a high degree of accuracy is essential.

Floating-Point Numbers

Representing a floating-point number on a computer presents a number of interesting challenges: the sign of the number must be preserved, the position of the decimal point must be saved, and the number itself must be saved. As with almost all other aspects of computer programming there is a variety of methods for representing a floating-point number. The most commonly used method on an 8088-based computer is the Institute of Electrical and Electronic Engineers (IEEE) floating-point format. This is the format that is used by most compilers and the 8088-related math coprocessors. To better understand how floating-point numbers are stored, take a look at the IEEE s**hort real format**.

The IEEE short real format requires 32 bits of storage space. The first step in storing a floating-point number using the short real format is to **normalize** it. Normalizing means that the binary representation of the floating-point number is shifted left or right until the first 1 in the number is positioned to the right of the binary point. This fractional part is called the **mantissa** and is stored as a 23-bit value. The number of positions the number was shifted is called the **exponent**. The exponent is **biased** by adding a 128 to the number shifts. Then the biased exponent is saved as an 8-bit value. Finally, the sign of the floating-point number is saved as a single bit just like it would be for a signed integer. Figure 3-10 illustrates how an IEEE short real is stored as a 32-bit value.

```
3 3 2 2 2 2 2 2 2 2 2 2 1 1 1 1 1 1 1 1 1 1
1 0 9 8 7 6 5 4 3 2 1 0 9 8 7 6 5 4 3 2 1 0 9 8 7 6 5 4 3 2 1 0
┌─┬─┬─┬─┬─┬─┬─┬─┬─┬─┬─┬─┬─┬─┬─┬─┬─┬─┬─┬─┬─┬─┬─┬─┬─┬─┬─┬─┬─┬─┬─┬─┐
│S│E│E│E│E│E│E│E│M│M│M│M│M│M│M│M│M│M│M│M│M│M│M│M│M│M│M│M│M│M│M│M│
└─┴─┴─┴─┴─┴─┴─┴─┴─┴─┴─┴─┴─┴─┴─┴─┴─┴─┴─┴─┴─┴─┴─┴─┴─┴─┴─┴─┴─┴─┴─┴─┘
```

Where:

```
S       is a sign bit.

E       is an exponent bit.

M       is a mantissa bit.
```

Figure 3-10. IEEE Short Real Floating-Point Format.

Characters and Strings

Perhaps the most important data an assembly language program handles are characters and strings. The program uses characters to communicate with you either on a video display or through a hard copy printout. Strings are just sequences of characters that have been strung together to form messages. Since characters and strings are so important, it is essential that you fully understand how characters are stored in memory.

Character Representation

The easiest way to understand how characters are represented in memory is to think back to when you were a child. At one time or another, many of us used secret codes to write messages to a friend. Often these codes consisted of assigning a number to represent a letter of the alphabet. Anyone who had the key to the code could easily interpret the message by simply substituting the appropriate letters for the numeric code.

Basically, the computer uses the same process to handle characters. Each character is assigned a numeric value. When it's time to either display the character on a video display or to print the character on a printer, the computer, the video display, and the printer are able to appropriately handle the character by looking up the value of the character in a table of codes.

ASCII Characters

The IBM PC uses the American Standard Code for Information Interchange (ASCII) character code table. Appendix A presents the complete list of the ASCII codes. As you can see from the table in Appendix A, the ASCII codes only define codes for the values in the range of 0 to 127. The values from 128 to 255 are not addressed by the ASCII table and must be defined by individual computer manufacturers. In the case of the IBM PC, the codes 128 to 255 are used for characters, such as, the PC's extended character set of line drawing characters or foreign language characters.

Since a byte can represent the values 0 to 255, a character is stored as a byte value in 8088 assembly language programming. A string of characters is stored as a series of byte values. Figure 3-11 illustrates how the string "8088" would be stored in memory.

```
   8    0    8    8
 ┌────┬────┬────┬────┐
 │3 8 │3 0 │3 8 │3 8 │
 └────┴────┴────┴────┘
```

Note:

These byte values are in hexadecimal.

Figure 3-11. How the String "8088" is Represented in Memory.

Summary

In this chapter, you learned how a wide variety of data types are represented in memory. These data types included integers, signed integers, Booleans, binary-coded decimals, floating-point numbers, characters, and strings. You also learned how these data types can be represented using the binary, decimal, and hexadecimal number systems.

Chapter 4

Working with Data

T hroughout an 8088 assembly language program, expressions define memory locations with the storage directives, values to be assigned to symbolic names with the assignment directives, and operand values. Both MASM and TASM have a very rich set of operators to make assigning these values easier. With these operators at your disposal, you can build complex expressions with ease. This chapter teaches you

- about directives, constants, and operators
- how to build expressions using these tools.

Directives

The 8088 assembly language directives enable you to create data values in an assembly language program.

The DB Directive

The DB (define byte) directive initializes a location of memory with a byte value. The range of values that can be stored as a byte are unsigned integers from 0 to 255 or signed integers from –128 to 127. The following example illustrates the syntax that is used to define a byte with the DB directive:

```
label          db      initializer,initializer,initializer
Where:
label                  is an optional label.
initializer            is an initial value for the memory
                       location. If an initializer of ? is
                       used, the memory location will have an
                       undefined initial value. When multiple
                       initial values are specified, they must
                       be separated by commas.
```

The following example shows some assembly language statements that use the **DB** directive to define bytes:

```
            .
            .
a           db      33
scores      db      98,99,100,95,92
hotkey      db      'A'
name        db      "Mark Goodwin"
array       db      10 dup (0)
            .
            .
```

Although the first two statements are rather self-explanatory, the last three need a little further explanation. The first of the last three statements is an example of how to define a character. You simply enclose the desired character in either apostrophes (') or quotes ("). The next assembly language statement illustrates how a string is defined. Like a character constant, you must enclose a string constant in either apostrophes (') or quotes ("). The last of the previous examples shows how an array or buffer is defined in memory. The **DUP** operator tells the assembler to **dup**licate one or more values in memory for a specified number of times. The following example illustrates how you use the **DUP** operator in an 8088 assembly language program:

```
count           dup   initializer,initializer,initializer
Where:
count                 is the number of times to duplicate the
                      initializer(s).
initializer           is one or more initial values. When
                      multiple initial values are specified,
                      they must be separated by commas.
```

The DW Directive

The **DW** (**define word**) directive initializes a location of memory with a word value. The range of values that can be stored as a word are unsigned integers from 0 to 65,545 or signed integers from −32,768 to 32,767. Besides being used to store integers, words are often used to store near pointers (segment offsets). The following example illustrates the syntax that is used to define a word with the **DW** directive:

```
label           dw    initializer,initializer,initializer
Where:
label                 is an optional label.
initializer           is one or more initial values. When
                      multiple initial values are specified,
                      they must be separated by commas.
```

The following example shows some assembly language statements that use the DW directive to define words:

```
                    .
                    .
account         dw      10000
count           dw      0ffffh
                    .
                    .
```

The DD Directive

The **DD** (**d**efine **d**oubleword) directive initializes a location of memory with a doubleword value. The range of values that can be stored as doublewords are unsigned integers from 0 to 4,294,967,295 or signed integers from −2,147,483,648 to 2,147,483,647. Besides being used to store extremely large integers, doublewords are often used to store far pointers (pointers that require both a segment address and a segment offset). The following example illustrates the syntax that defines a doubleword with the **DD** directive:

```
    label           dd      initializer,initializer,initializer
Where:
    label                   is an optional label.
    initializer             is one or more initial values. When
                            multiple initial values are specified,
                            they must be separated by commas.
```

The DQ Directive

The **DQ** (**d**efine **q**uadword) directive initializes a location of memory with a 64-bit value. Quadwords are commonly used to store floating-point values. The following example illustrates the syntax that defines a 64-bit value with the **DQ** directive:

```
label            dq     initializer,initializer,initializer
Where:
label                   is an optional label.
initializer             is one or more initial values. When
                        more than one initial value is speci-
                        fied, they must be separated by commas.
```

The DT Directive

The **DT** (**d**efine **t**enbyte) directive initializes a location of memory with an 80-bit value. By default, the **DT** directive defines binary-coded decimals that are 10 bytes in length. The following example illustrates the syntax that defines an 80-bit value with the **DT** directive:

```
label            dt     initializer,initializer,initializer
Where:
label                   is an optional label.
initializer             is one or more initial values. When
                        multiple initial values are specified,
                        they must be separated by commas.
```

The EQU Directive

The **EQU** (**equ**ate) directive assigns the result of an integer expression, a previously defined symbol, or an assembler symbol to a symbolic name.

The assembler replaces the symbolic name with its assigned value. The following example illustrates the syntax for assigning a value to a symbolic name with the **EQU** directive:

```
label              equ    value
Where:
label                     is the symbolic name to be assigned.
value                     is the value to be assigned to the
                          symbolic name.
```

The following example shows some assembly language statements that use the **EQU** directive to assign values to a symbolic name:

```
            .
            .
row     equ    [bp+2]
copy    equ    mov
length  equ    3*55
            .
            .
```

The = Directive

The = (equals) directive assigns the result of an integer expression, a previously defined symbol, or an assembler symbol to a symbolic name.

Although the = directive and the **EQU** directive seem identical, they have one important difference. The value assigned by an **EQU** directive cannot be changed; however, the value assigned by the = directive can be changed throughout the program. The following example illustrates the syntax for assigning a value to a symbolic name with the = directive:

```
label          =       value
Where:
label                  is the symbolic name to be assigned.
value                  is the value to be assigned to the
                       symbolic name.
```

Constants

When building an expression, many numeric constants are required. By default, the assembler assumes that all constants are decimal numbers. To properly translate numeric constants of other bases, a **radix** specifier must be added to the end of the numeric constant. The following example illustrates the radix specifiers that are offered by MASM and TASM:

Radix	Specifier
Binary	B or b
Octal	Q, q, O, or O
Decimal	D or d
Hexadecimal	H or h

Note: The previous example refers to the octal number system. The octal number system is base 8 and was once widely used in assembly language programs. That number system is rarely used today; therefore it is not covered in this book.

There is one other requirement for constructing numeric constants that you must be aware of: All numeric constants must start with one of the digits 0 to 9. By starting with a numeric digit, the assembler immediately knows that it is a numeric constant and not a symbolic name. Although this requirement does not affect binary, octal, or decimal numbers, many hexadecimal numbers start with a letter. Luckily, this assembler rule can be complied with quite easily by preceding all hexadecimal constants whose first digit is a letter with a 0. For example, the value FE_{16} would be written as 0feh and not feh.

The .RADIX Directive

The **.RADIX** directive changes the default radix from decimal to any number base from 2 to 16. The following example illustrates the syntax for changing the assembler's default radix with the **.RADIX** directive:

```
.radix  expression
```

Where:

expression   is the value of the new default number
                            base. Note that the expression is
                            always considered to be decimal.

Operators

Operators express the relationship of one data value to another in assembly language programs.

The + Operator

The + operator returns the result of adding one expression with another. The following example illustrates the syntax for adding together two expression with the + operator:

```
expression + expression
```

Where:

expression   is a valid expression

The following example shows some expressions that use the + operator:

```
          .
          .
a         db      33 + 16
b         db      44 + 14
          .
          .
```

The – Operator

The – operator returns the result of subtracting one expression from another. The following example illustrates the syntax for subtracting one expression from another using the – operator:

```
expression  -  expression
```
Where:
```
expression      is a valid expression
```

The following example shows some expressions that use the – operator:

```
          .
          .
a         db      55 - 33
b         db      66 - 100
          .
          .
```

The * Operator

The * operator returns the result of multiplying one expression with another. The following example illustrates the syntax for multiplying together two expressions with the * operator:

```
expression * expression
```

Where:

```
expression    is a valid expression.
```

The following example shows some expressions that use the * operator:

```
            .
            .
a       dw      25 * 64
b       db      2 * 4
            .
            .
```

The / Operator

The / operator returns the result of dividing one expression by another. The following example illustrates the syntax for dividing two expressions with the / operator:

```
expression / expression
```

Where:

```
expression    is a valid expression.
```

The following example shows some expressions that use the / operator:

```
        •

        •

a       db      66 / 2
b       dw      44 / 10

        •

        •
```

The MOD Operator

The **MOD** operator returns the remainder of dividing one expression by another. The following example illustrates the syntax for calculating the remainder of dividing two expressions with the **MOD** operator:

```
expression  mod  expression
Where:
expression    is a valid expression.
```

The following example shows some expressions that use the mod operator:

```
        •

        •

a       db      33 mod 10
b       db      20 mod 18

        •

        •
```

The NOT Operator

The **NOT** operator inverts the values of the bits of an expression. The following table is a truth table for the **NOT** operator. As the table shows, the **NOT** operator changes any bits equal to 1 to 0 and changes any bits equal to 0 to 1.

Bit	NOT Bit
1	0
0	1

The following example illustrates the syntax for inverting an expression with the **NOT** operator:

```
not expression
```
Where:
```
expression    is a valid expression.
```

The following example shows some expressions that use the **NOT** operator:

```
        .
        .
a       db    not 01110110b
b       db    not 3
        .
        .
```

The AND Operator

The **AND** operator can bitwise and one expression with another. The following example presents a truth table for the **AND** operator. As this table shows, the **AND** operator returns a 1 in each bit position of the result if both of the corresponding bit positions in the two expressions are both equal to 1. Otherwise, the **AND** operator returns a 0 in the appropriate bit position.

Y	Y	X AND Y
1	1	1
1	0	0
0	1	0
0	0	0

The following example illustrates the syntax for anding one expression with another:

```
expression and expression
Where:
expression    is a valid expression.
```

The following example shows some expressions that use the **AND** operator:

```
        .
        .
a    db    01110110b and 10100101b
b    db    0feh and 35
        .
        .
```

The OR Operator

The **OR** operator can bitwise or one expression with another. The following table is a truth table for the **OR** operator. As this table shows, the **OR** operator returns a 1 in each bit position of the result if either of the corresponding bit positions in the two expressions are equal to 1. Otherwise, the **OR** operator returns a 0 in the appropriate bit position.

X	Y	X OR Y
1	1	1
1	0	1
0	1	1
0	0	0

The following example illustrates the syntax for oring one expression with another:

```
expression or expression
```
Where:
```
expression    is a valid expression.
```

The following example shows some expressions that use the or operator:

```
        .
        .
a    db    10001101b or 00010001b
b    db    10000111b or 13h
        .
        .
```

The XOR Operator

The **XOR** operator performs a bitwise exclusive or on two expressions. The following table is a truth table for the **XOR** operator. As this table shows, the **XOR** operator returns 1 in each bit position of the result if only one of the corresponding bit positions in the two expressions is equal to 1. Otherwise, the **XOR** operator returns a 0 in the appropriate bit position.

X	Y	X XOR Y
1	1	0
1	0	1
0	1	1
0	0	0

The following example illustrates the syntax for exclusive oring one expression with another:

```
expression xor expression
Where:
expression    is a valid expression.
```

The following example shows some expressions that use the **XOR** operator:

```
          .
          .
          .
a      db      01110111b xor 10101010b
b      db      10101010b xor 0ffh
          .
          .
```

The SHL Operator

The **SHL** operator **sh**ifts **l**eft the bits of one expression by the number of bits indicated in another expression. Note that with each shift, the most significant bit is lost and the least significant bit is set to 0. If the most significant bit of the expression was a 0, this has the effect of multiplying the expression by 2 for each shift. The following example illustrates the syntax for shifting an expression to the left with the **SHL** operator:

```
expression shl count
Where:
expression          is a valid expression.
count               is the number of times to shift the
                    expression to the left.
```

The following example shows some expressions that use the **SHL** operator:

```
        .
        .
a       db      01001011b shl 3
b       db      3ah shl 1
        .
        .
```

The SHR Operator

The **SHR** operator **sh**ifts **r**ight the bits of one expression by the number of bits indicated in another expression. Note that with each shift, the least significant bit is lost and the most significant bit is set to 0. This has the effect of dividing the expression by 2 for each shift. The following example illustrates the syntax for shifting an expression to the right with the **SHR** operator:

```
expression shr count
Where:
expression          is a valid expression.
count               is the number of times to shift the
                    expression to the right.
```

The following example shows some expressions that use the **SHR** operator:

```
            .
            .
a       db      11110101 shr 4
b       db      43 shr 1
            .
            .
```

The EQ Operator

The **EQ** operator determines if one expression is **equal** to another expression. If the expressions are equal, the **EQ** operator returns a value of True (1). Otherwise, the **EQ** operator returns a value of False (0) to indicate the expressions are not equal. The following example illustrates the syntax for testing two expressions with the **EQ** operator:

```
expression eq expression
```
Where:
```
expression    is a valid expression.
```

The following example shows some expressions that use the **EQ** operator:

```
            .
            .
a       db      43 eq 41
b       db      41 eq 41
            .
            .
```

The NE Operator

The **NE** operator determines if one expression is **not** equal to another expression. If the expressions are not equal, the **NE** operator returns a value of True (1). Otherwise, the **NE** operator returns a value of False (0) to indicate the expressions are equal. The following example illustrates the syntax for testing two expressions with the **NE** operator:

```
expression ne expression
Where:
expression    is a valid expression.
```

The following example shows some expressions that use the **NE** operator:

```
          .
          .
a       db      43 ne 41
b       db      41 ne 41
          .
          .
```

The LT Operator

The **LT** operator determines if one expression is less than another expression. If the first expression is less than the second expression, the **LT** operator returns a value of True (1). Otherwise, the **LT** operator returns a value of False (0) to indicate that the first expression is either greater than or equal to the second expression. The following example illustrates the syntax for testing two expressions with the **LT** operator:

```
expression lt expression
Where:
expression    is a valid expression.
```

The following example shows some expressions that use the **LT** operator:

```
        .
        .
a       db      43 lt 41
b       db      41 lt 55
        .
        .
```

The LE Operator

The **LE** operator determines if one expression is less than or equal to another expression. If the first expression is less than or equal to the second expression, the **LE** operator returns a value of True (1). Otherwise, the **LE** operator returns a value of False (0) to indicate that the first expression is greater than the second expression. The following example illustrates the syntax for testing two expressions with the **LE** operator:

```
expression le expression
Where:
expression     is a valid expression.
```

The following example shows some expressions that use the **LE** operator:

```
        .
        .
a       db      43 le 41
b       db      41 le 43
        .
        .
```

The GT Operator

The **GT** operator determines if one expression is greater than another expression. If the first expression is greater than the second expression, the **GT** operator returns a value of True (1). Otherwise, the **GT** operator returns a value of False (0) to indicate that the first expression is either less than or equal to the second expression. The following example illustrates the syntax for testing two expressions with the **GT** operator:

```
expression gt expression
Where:
expression    is a valid expression.
```

The following example shows some expressions that use the **GT** operator:

```
            •
            •
a       db      43 gt 41
b       db      41 gt 55
            •
            •
```

The GE Operator

The **GE** operator determines if one expression is greater than or equal to another expression. If the first expression is greater than or equal to the second expression, the **GE** operator returns a value of True (1). Otherwise, the **GE** operator returns a value of False (0) to indicate that the first expression is less than the second expression. The following example illustrates the syntax for testing two expressions with the **GE** operator:

```
expression ge expression
Where:
expression    is a valid expression.
```

The following example shows some expressions that use the **GE** operator:

```
        .
        .
a       db      43 ge 41
b       db      41 ge 55
        .
        .
```

The SEG Operator

The **SEG** directive returns the **segment** address for an operand. The following example illustrates the syntax for determining the segment address of an operand using the **SEG** operator:

```
seg expression
Where:
expression              is a label, variable, segment name,
                        group name, or any other memory operand.
```

The following example shows an expression that uses the **SEG** operator:

```
        .
        .
a       db      ?
        .
        .
        mov   ax,seg a    ;AX=a's segment address
        .
        .
```

The OFFSET Operator

The **OFFSET** operator returns the memory offset where an operand resides in a segment. This memory offset is often referred to as a **near** pointer. The following example illustrates the syntax for determining the offset address of an operand using the **OFFSET** operator:

```
offset expression
Where:
expression              is a label, variable, or any other
                        memory operand.
```

The following example shows an expression that uses the **OFFSET** operator:

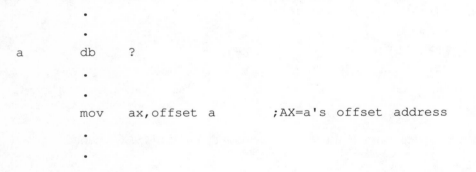

```
        .
        .
a       db    ?
        .
        .
        mov   ax,offset a          ;AX=a's offset address
        .
        .
```

The TYPE Operator

The **TYPE** operator returns the number of bytes for each data object that is in a variable. Additionally, the **TYPE** operator returns a value of 0ffffh for near labels (labels in the same segment) and 0fffeh for far labels (labels that are outside of the current segment). Finally, the **TYPE** operator returns a value of 0 for a constant. The following example illustrates how the **TYPE** operator determines data types:

```
type expression
Where:
expression              is a variable, a near label, a far
                        label, or a constant.
```

The following example shows some expressions that use the **TYPE** operator:

```
        .

        .

a       dw      1000
b       db      100 dup (?)

        .

        .

        mov     ax,type a    ;AX = 2
        mov     bx,type b    ;BX = 1

        .

        .
```

The LENGTH Operator

The **LENGTH** operator returns the number of data objects in a variable. The following example illustrates the syntax for determining the number of elements in a variable with the **LENGTH** operator:

```
length variable
Where:
variable            is a previously defined variable.
```

The following example shows some expressions that use the **LENGTH** operator:

```
        •
        •
a       db      50 dup (?)
buffer  dw      100 dup (0)
c       db      10
        •
        •

        mov     ax,length a         ;AX = 50
        mov     bx,length buffer    ;BX = 100
        mov     cx,length c         ;CX = 1
        •
        •
```

The SIZE Operator

The **SIZE** operator returns the number of bytes the assembler allocates for a variable. Essentially, this can also be determined by multiplying the variable's **TYPE** by its **LENGTH**. The following example illustrates the syntax for determining the number of bytes in a variable:

```
size variable
Where:
variable            is a previously defined variable.
```

The following example shows some expressions that use the **SIZE** operator:

```
          .
          .

a         db      50 dup (?)
buffer    dw      100 dup (0)
c         db      10
          .
          .
          mov     ax,size a          ;AX = 50
          mov     bx,size buffer     ;BX = 200
          mov     cx,size c          ;CX = 1
          .
          .
```

The HIGH Operator

The **HIGH** operator returns the high-order eight bits of a constant expression. The following example illustrates the syntax for determining the high-order eight bits of a constant expression with the **HIGH** operator:

```
high expression
Where:
expression          is an expression with a value that
                    never changes.
```

The following example shows an expression that uses the **HIGH** operator:

```
        •
        •
a       equ   0f3e5h
        •
        •
        mov   ah,high a    ;AH = 0f3h
        •
        •
```

The LOW Operator

The **LOW** operator returns the low-order eight bits of a constant expression. The following example illustrates the syntax for determining the low-order eight bits of a constant expression with the **LOW** operator:

```
low expression
```
Where:

expression   is an expression with a value that
                        never changes.

The following example shows an expression that uses the **LOW** operator:

```
        •
        •
a       equ   0f3e5h
        •
        •
        mov   ah,low a     ;AH = 0e5h
        •
        •
```

The PTR Operator

The **PTR** operator forces an expression to a specified type. The following example illustrates the syntax for forcing an expression to a specified type with the **PTR** operator:

```
type ptr expression
```

Where:

type   is **BYTE, WORD, DWORD, FWORD, QWORD,** or **TBYTE** for memory
            operands or **NEAR, FAR,** or **PROC** for labels.

expression is a valid memory operand or label.

The following example shows an expression that uses the **PTR** operator:

```
        .
        .
a       dw    300
        .
        .
        mov   al,byte ptr a      ;AL = a's low-order byte
        .
        .
```

The Segment-Override Operators

The **segment-override** operators force an address to be relative to the specified segment. The 8088 registers are all associated with a default segment. The segment-override operators enable you to override these assumptions. The following example illustrates the syntax for overriding the assumed segment for an address with a segment-override operator:

```
segment:expression
```
Where:
```
segment           is either CS, DS, SS, or ES.
expression        is the address of a variable or label.
```

The following example shows an expression that uses a segment-override operator:

```
    .
    .
    .
mov    ax,ss:[bx+8]        ;[BX + 8] is now assumed to
                           ; be in the SS segment
    .
    .
    .
```

Operator Precedence

So far in this chapter, all of the expressions have used only one operator to form an expression. Consequently, there is little doubt about the values that the expressions return. But what about expressions that have more than one operator?

An expression that has multiple instances of the same operator is evaluated on a strictly left-to-right basis. Look at how the expression **3 + 4 + 5** is evaluated. First, the subexpression **3 + 4** is evaluated and returns **7**. This leaves the remainder of the expression to be evaluated as **7 + 5**, which returns a result of **12**.

Expressions that are built from subexpressions with different operators use precedence rules to determine the correct result. Look at how the expression **3 + 4 * 5** would be evaluated. If the assembler evaluates the subexpression **3 + 4** first, the result would be **35**. If the assembler evaluates the subexpression **4 * 5** first, the result will be **23**. Obviously, there has to be a set of rules to evaluate expressions to prevent chaotic results. This is where the precedence rules of the assembler come into play.

The following example illustrates the precedence levels for the operators that have been discussed so far:

LENGTH	**SIZE**					
segment-override		**PTR**	**OFFSET**		**SEG**	**TYPE**
HIGH	**LOW**					
*	/	**MOD**	**SHL**		**SHR**	
+	–					
EQ	**NE**	**LT**	**LE**		**GT**	**GE**
NOT						
AND						
OR	**XOR**					
SHORT						

When the assembler evaluates an expression with multiple operators, it first evaluates the subexpressions with the highest precedence (relative to their positions in the Operator Precedence table) first. If there is more than one subexpression with operators of equal precedence, the assembler evaluates the subexpressions on a left-to-right basis. By applying these precedence rules, it's easy to determine that the expression **3 + 4 * 5** would result in **23** and not **35**. The reason for this is that the * operator has a higher precedence than the + operator. The operator precedence rules can be overridden by using parenthesis. For example, the expression **(3 + 4) * 5** returns a result of **35**.

The Location Counter

The location counter ($) is a special operand that returns the address of the statement that is being assembled. The following example shows an expression that uses the location counter ($):

```
        .

        .

string  db    "This is a sample string"
strlen  equ   $-string   ;strlen = the length of string
        .

        .
```

Summary

In this chapter, you learned about data storage directives and data assignment directives. Additionally, this chapter introduced you to the assembly language operators and how they are used to build expressions. Finally, you learned how the location counter retrieves the current address.

Chapter 5

The 8088
Instruction Set

T his chapter teaches you about the all important 8088 instruction set. You can use these instructions to construct the code segment of your assembly language program. You will get a detailed look at many of the most important 8088 operation codes (opcodes). These opcodes can be classed as

- data movement instructions
- arithmetic instructions
- data conversion instructions
- bit string and Boolean instructions
- program control and iteration instructions
- flag instructions.

Additionally, there are a few other miscellaneous instructions.

An Assembly Language Instruction

Most assembly language instructions have two basic parts: the operation and the operands. Although every assembly language instruction has to have an operation, not all assembly language instructions have operands. To simplify the explanations for the instructions, this book uses the following notations to describe operands in a general manner:

Reg	A register.
Reg8	An 8-bit register: **AL**, **AH**, **BL**, **BH**, **CL**, **CH**, **DL**, or **DH**.
Reg16	A 16-bit general purpose register: **AX**, **BX**, **CX**, **DX**, **SP**, **BP**, **SI**, or **DI**.
SReg	A segment register: **CS**, **DS**, **ES**, or **SS**.
Mem	A memory location.
Mem8	An 8-bit memory location.
Mem16	A 16-bit memory location.
Imm	An immediate value. In other words, any specific value like an integer or a previously defined symbol.
Imm8	An 8-bit immediate value.
Imm16	A 16-bit immediate value.

Data Movement Instructions

Data movement instructions perform the following tasks:

- Move data between the 8088 registers and the computer memory

- Exchange data between registers and memory

- Access a specified element in a byte array

- Load a near pointer into a register

- Load far pointers into either the **DS** or **ES** registers and a specified 16-bit register.

The MOV Instruction

The 8088 **MOV** (**move**) instruction moves data between registers and memory. The following example defines the syntax for the **MOV** instruction:

```
mov             destination,source
```

Where:

destination   is a Reg8, Reg16, SReg, Mem8, or Mem16.

source   is a Reg8, Reg16, SReg, Mem8, Mem16, or Imm.

Notes:

You cannot use CS as the destination. A memory location cannot be both the destination and the source. An immediate value cannot be used if the destination is a segment register.

The following example shows some statements that use the 8088 **MOV** instruction:

```
        .
        .
mov     ax,4    ;AX = 4
mov     si,dx   ;SI = DX
        .
        .
```

The XCHG Instruction

The 8088 **XCHG** (ex**chang**e) instruction swaps the contents of two registers or a register and a memory location. The following example defines the syntax for the **XCHG** instruction:

```
xchg            operand,operand
Where:
operand         is a Reg8, Reg16, Mem8, or Mem16.

Notes:

Although both operands can be registers, only one operand
can be a memory location. Furthermore, the data values
being swapped must be of the same size, for example, Reg8<-
>Reg8, Reg16<->Reg16, Reg8<->Mem8, Reg16<->Mem16.
```

The following example shows an assembly language statement that uses the **XCHG** instruction:

```
        .
        .
a   db    20
        .
        .
    xchg   ah,a    ;Exchange the contents of AH
                   ; with a
        .
        .
```

The LDS Instruction

The **LDS** (load **DS**) instruction moves a far pointer (a segment and an offset address) into segment register **DS** and another 16-bit register. Upon completion of the instruction, segment register **DS** holds the segment address and the specified 16-bit register holds the offset address. The following example defines the syntax for the **LDS** instruction:

```
lds           Reg16,Mem32
Where:
Reg16                 is the register that will hold the
                      offset address.
Mem32                 is the location in memory that holds
                      the far pointer.
```

The following example shows an assembly language statement that uses the **LDS** instruction:

```
        .
        .
a    db     (?)
aptr equ    this dword
     dw     offset a
     dw     seg    a
        .
        .
     lds    si,aptr              ;DS:SI = a's address
        .
        .
```

Note in the above example, the use of the **THIS** operator. The **THIS** operator defines the type for a label. In this case, the **THIS** operator creates a label for a doubleword variable.

The LES Instruction

The **LES** (load **ES**) instruction moves a far pointer (a segment and an offset address) into segment register **ES** and another 16-bit register. Upon completion of the instruction, segment register **ES** holds the segment address and the specified 16-bit register holds the offset address. The following example defines the syntax for the **LES** instruction:

```
les           Reg16,Mem32
Where:
Reg16                    is the register that will hold the
                         offset address.

Mem32                    is the location in memory that holds
                         the far pointer.
```

The following example shows an assembly language statement that uses the **LES** instruction:

```
      .
      .
a     db      (?)
aptr  equ     this dword
      dw      offset a
      dw      segment a
      .
      .
      les     di,aptr                ;ES:DI = a's address
      .
      .
```

The LEA Instruction

The **LEA** (load effective address) instruction moves an offset address into a 16-bit register. The following example defines the syntax for using the **LEA** instruction:

```
lea           Reg16,Mem16
Where:
Reg16                    is the register that will hold the
                         offset address.
Mem16                    is the memory address to be loaded into
                         the register.
```

The following example shows an assembly language statement that uses the **LEA** instruction:

```
        .
        .
a    db      (?)
        .
        .
     lea    bx,a    ;BX = a's address
        .
        .
```

The XLAT Instruction

The **XLAT** (translate) instruction moves an array element into register **AL**. Before the instruction is called, register **BX** holds the starting address of the array and register **AL** holds the element number −1. The following example defines the syntax for the **XLAT** instruction:

xlat   array

Where:

array   is the address of the array to be
                  translated. Note that this operand is
                  optional and is only necessary when a
                  segment override is specified.

The following example shows an assembly language statement that uses the **XLAT** instruction:

```
        .
        .
a   db      3,4,6,10,11
        .
        .
    mov     al,1                    ;Specify the 2nd element
    mov     bx,offset a             ;BX = Array's address
    xlat                            ;Move the 2nd element into
                                    ; AL
        .
        .
```

The Arithmetic Instructions

The 8088 has a rich set of arithmetic instructions. The 8088 arithmetic instructions perform such operations as incrementing, decrementing, negating, adding, subtracting, multiplying and dividing.

The INC Instruction

The **INC** (**inc**rement) instruction increases the value of a register or a memory location by 1. The following example defines the syntax for the **INC** instruction:

```
inc             operand
Where:
operand             is a Reg8, Reg16, Mem8, or Mem16.
```

The following example shows some assembly language statements that use the **INC** instruction:

```
        .
        .
a    db      1
b    dw      33
        .
        .
     inc    al        ;Increment AL
     inc    a         ;Increment memory location a
     inc    cx        ;Increment CX
     inc    b         ;Increment memory location b
        .
        .
```

The DEC Instruction

The **DEC** (**decrement**) instruction decreases the value of a register or a memory location by 1. The following example defines the syntax for the **DEC** instruction:

```
dec              operand
Where:
operand                  is a Reg8, Reg16, Mem8, or Mem16.
```

The following example shows some assembly language statements that use the **DEC** instruction:

```
        .
        .
a   db      1
b   dw      33
        .
        .
    dec     al      ;Decrement AL
    dec     a       ;Decrement memory location a
    dec     cx      ;Decrement CX
    dec     b       ;Decrement b
        .
        .
```

The NEG Instruction

The **NEG** (**neg**ate) instruction inverts the sign of a register or memory location. The **NEG** instruction performs this task by doing a 2's complement on the operand. The following example defines the syntax for the **NEG** instruction:

```
neg             operand
Where:
operand                 is a Reg8, Reg16, Mem8, or Mem16.
```

The following example shows some assembly language statements that use the **NEG** instruction:

```
         .
         .
a    db      -3
         .
         .
     mov     ax,45     ;AX = 45
     neg     ax        ;AX = -45
     neg     a         ;a = 3
         .
         .
```

The ADD Instruction

The **ADD** (**add**ition) instruction adds the value of one operand to another. The following example defines the syntax for the **ADD** instruction:

add   destination,source

Where:

destination   is the register or memory location that holds one of the operands and will hold the result of the operation. The destination operand can be a Reg8, Reg16,Mem8, or Mem16.

source   is a register, memory location, or immediate value to be added to the destination operand. The source operand can be a Reg8, Reg16, Mem8, Mem16, Imm8, or Imm16.

Notes:

Although both the destination and the source operands can be registers, only one operand at a time can be a memory location. Additionally, immediate values are only allowed for source operands.

The following example shows some assembly language statements that use the **ADD** instruction:

```
        .
        .
a    db      3
b    dw      45
        .
        .
     add    ax,345   ;AX = AX + 345
     add    a,35     ;a = a + 35
     add    b,cx     ;b = b + CX
     add    dx,b     ;DX = DX + b
        .
        .
```

The ADC Instruction

The **ADC** (**ad**d with **c**arry) instruction adds the value of one operand and the value of the **carry** flag to another operand. Whenever a previous addition operation (either **ADD** or **ADC**) overflows the destination operand, the **carry** flag is set to 1. Basically, the **ADC** instruction is used in conjunction with the **ADD** instruction to add together two values that are greater than two bytes in length.

Suppose you wanted to add together two 32-bit values. The two values could be correctly added together by first adding together the least significant 16 bits for both values with the **ADD** instruction. The addition operation would be completed by adding the most significant 16 bits and the **carry** flag with the **ADC** instruction. The reason for using the **ADC** instruction instead of another **ADD** instruction is that the result of adding the least significant 16 bits could be larger than 16 bits; thus, setting the **carry** flag. Even larger values can use this same method by using successive **ADC** instructions on the more significant bits. Just remember to use the **ADD** instruction on the least significant bits, and then always use the **ADC** instruction for the remainder of the operation. The following example defines the syntax for the **ADC** instruction:

```
adc            destination,source
Where:
destination            is the register or memory location that
                       holds one of the operands and will hold
                       the result of the operation. The desti-
                       nation operand can be a Reg8, Reg16,
                       Mem8, or Mem16.

source                 is a register, memory location, or
                       immediate value to be added to the
                       destination operand. The source operand
                       can be a Reg8, Reg16, Mem8, Mem16,
                       Imm8, or Imm16.
```

Notes:

```
Although both the destination and the source operands can
be registers, only one operand at a time can be a memory
location. Additionally, immediate values are only allowed
for source operands.
```

The following example shows an assembly language instruction that uses the **ADC** instruction:

```
        .
        .
    mov     ax,345          ;AX = Least significant
                            ; 16 bits
    add     ax,33000        ;AX = Result's least
                            ; significant 16 bits
    mov     dx,50000        ;DX = Most significant
                            ; 16 bits
    adc     dx,5534         ;DX:AX = 32-bit result
        .
        .
```

The SUB Instruction

The **SUB** (**sub**tract) instruction subtracts the value of one operand from another. The following example defines the syntax for the **SUB** instruction:

sub   destination,source

Where:

destination   is the register or memory location that holds the value that the source operand is to be subtracted from. Additionally, the destination operand will hold the result of the operation. The destination operand can be a Reg8, Reg16, Mem8, or Mem16.

source   is a register, memory location, or immediate value to be subtracted from the destination operand. The source can be a Reg8, Reg16, Mem8, Mem16, Imm8, or Imm16.

Notes:

Although both the destination and the source operands can be registers, only one operand at a time can be a memory location. Additionally, immediate values are only allowed for source operands.

The following example shows some assembly language statements that use the **SUB** instruction:

```
        .
        .
a    db    3
b    dw    35
        .
        .
     sub    ax,345   ;AX = AX - 345
     sub    a,35     ;a = a - 35
     sub    b,cx     ;b = b - cx
     sub    dx,b     ;DX = DX - b
        .
        .
```

The SBB Instruction

The **SBB** (subtract with borrow) instruction subtracts the value of one operand and the value of the **carry** flag from another operand. Whenever a previous subtraction operation (either **SUB** or **SBB**) underflows the destination operand, the **carry** flag is set to 1. Much like the **ADD/ADC** combination of instructions adds together values larger than 16 bits, the **SUB/SBB** combination subtracts values larger than 16 bits. Assume that you need to subtract two 32-bit values. The two least significant 16-bit values would be subtracted with the **SUB** instruction. The operation would continue by subtracting the most significant 16-bit values and the **carry** flag with the **SBB** instruction. With subtraction operations on values with more than 32-bits, just continue to subtract with the **SBB** instruction. The following example defines the syntax for the **SBB** instruction:

sbb   destination,source

Where:

destination   is the register or memory location that holds the value that the source operand is to be subtracted from. Additionally, the destination operand will hold the result of the operation. The destination operand can be a Reg8, Reg16, Mem8, or Mem16.

source   is a register, memory location, or immediate value to be subtracted from the destination operand. The source can be a Reg8, Reg16, Mem8, Mem16, Imm8, or Imm16.

Notes:

Although both the destination and the source operands can be registers, only one operand at a time can be a memory location. Additionally, immediate values are only allowed for source operands.

The following example shows some assembly language statements that use the **SBB** instruction:

```
        .
        .
mov     ax,10000        ;AX = Least significant
                        ; 16 bits
sub     ax,20000        ;AX = Result's least
                        ; significant 16 bits
mov     dx,50000        ;DX = Most significant
                        ; 16 bits
sbb     dx,32000        ;DX:AX = 32-bit result
        .
        .
```

The MUL Instruction

The **MUL** (**mul**tiply) instruction multiplies either an unsigned byte or word by another unsigned byte or word. The following example defines the syntax for the **MUL** instruction:

```
mul           operand
```

Where:

operand   is either a Reg8 or Mem8 for multiplying unsigned bytes or Reg16 or Mem16 for multiplying unsigned words.

Notes:

When multiplying unsigned bytes, the contents of register **AL** are multiplied by the operand and the result is returned in registers **AH** and **AL**. When multiplying unsigned words, the contents of register **AX** are multiplied by the operand and the result is returned in registers **DX** and **AX**.

The following example shows some assembly language statements that use the **MUL** instruction:

```
        •
        •
a   dw      45
        •
        •
    mov     ax,35000            ;AX = 35000
    mul     a                   ;DX:AX = 32-bit result of
                                ; 35000 * 45
        •
        •
```

The IMUL Instruction

The **IMUL** (signed **int**eger **mul**tiplication) instruction multiplies either a signed byte or word by another signed byte or word. The following example defines the syntax for the **IMUL** instruction:

```
imul          operand
```

Where:

operand   is either a Reg8 or Mem8 for multiply-
                       ing signed bytes or Reg16 or Mem16 for
                       multiplying signed words.

Notes:

When multiplying signed bytes, the contents of register **AL** is multiplied by the operand and the result is returned in registers **AH** and **AL**. When multiplying signed words, the contents of register **AX** is multiplied by the operand and the result is returned in registers **DX** and **AX**.

The following example shows some assembly language statements that use the **IMUL** instruction:

```
        .
        .
a    dw      -45
        .
        .
     mov    ax,35000            ;AX = 35000
     imul   a                   ;DX:AX = 32-bit result of
                                ; 35000 * -45
        .
        .
```

The DIV Instruction

The **DIV** (**div**ision) instruction either divides an unsigned word by an unsigned byte or an unsigned doubleword by an unsigned word. The following example defines the syntax for the **DIV** instruction:

div   operand

Where:

operand   is a Reg8 or Mem8 divisor for dividing an unsigned word by an unsigned byte or a Reg16 or Mem16 divisor for dividing an unsigned doubleword by an unsigned word.

Notes:

When dividing an unsigned word by an unsigned byte, the dividend must be placed in **AX** before executing the **DIV** instruction. Upon completion of the operation, the quotient is returned in register **AL** and the remainder is returned in register **AH**.

When dividing an unsigned doubleword by an unsigned word, the dividend must be placed in **DX** and **AX** before executing the **DIV** instruction. **DX** will hold the doubleword's most significant 16 bits and **AX** will hold the doubleword's least significant 16 bits. Upon completion of the operation, the quotient is returned in register **AX** and the remainder is returned in register **DX**.

Whenever the divisor is equal to 0, the 8088 aborts the program and displays a divide overflow error message. Accordingly, a properly structured program should check for divide by 0 errors before they occur.

The following example shows some assembly language statements that use the **DIV** instruction:

```
        .
        .
a    db       3
        .
        .
     mov     ax,35    ;AX = Dividend
     div     a        ;Divide AX by a
        .
        .
```

The IDIV Instruction

The **IDIV** (signed integer division) instruction either divides a signed word by a signed byte or a signed doubleword by a signed word. The following example defines the syntax for the **IDIV** instruction:

```
idiv             operand
```

Where:

operand   is a Reg8 or Mem8 divisor for dividing
                           a signed word by a signed byte or a
                           Reg16 or Mem16 divisor for dividing a
                           signed doubleword by a signed word.

Notes:

When dividing a signed word by a signed byte, the dividend must be placed in **AX** before executing the **IDIV** instruction. Upon completion of the operation, the quotient is returned in register **AL** and the remainder is returned in register **AH**.

When dividing a signed doubleword by a signed word, the dividend must be placed in **DX** and **AX** before executing the **IDIV** instruction. **DX** will hold the doubleword's most significant 16 bits and **AX** will hold the doubleword's least significant 16 bits. Upon completion of the operation, the quotient is returned in register **AX** and the remainder is returned in register **DX**.

Whenever the divisor is equal to 0, the 8088 aborts the program and displays a divide overflow error message. Accordingly, a properly structured program should check for divide-by 0 errors before they occur.

The following example shows some assembly language statements that use the **IDIV** instruction:

```
        .
        .
a       db      -4
        .
        .
        mov     ax,645   ;AX = Dividend
        idiv    a        ;Divide AX by a
        .
        .
```

Data Conversion Instructions

When performing arithmetic operations, the data to be processed is not always in the form that is required for the intended operation. Furthermore, the 8088 always assumes that arithmetic operations are being performed on binary integers. Consequently, the 8088 instruction set has conversion instructions that ensure correct results for binary-coded decimal operations.

The CBW Instruction

The **CBW** (convert **byte word**) instruction sign extends a byte in **AL** into a word in **AX**. Accordingly, register **AH** is set to 0 for a positive value in **AL** or 0FFH for a negative value in **AL**. The following example defines the syntax for the **CBW** instruction:

```
cbw
```

The following example shows some assembly language statements that use the **CBW** instruction:

```
        .
        .
mov     al,3              ;AL = 3
cbw                       ;AX = 3
mov     al,-50            ;AL = -50
cbw                       ;AX = -50
        .
        .
```

The CWD Instruction

The **CWD** (**c**onvert **w**ord to **d**oubleword) instruction sign extends the word in **AX** into a doubleword in **DX:AX**. Accordingly, register **DX** is set to 0 for a positive value in **AX** or 0FFFFH for a negative value in **AX**. The following example defines the syntax for the **CWD** instruction:

```
cwd
```

The following example shows some assembly language statements that use the **CWD** instruction:

```
        .
        .
mov     ax,-5304          ;AX = -5304
cwd                       ;DX:AX = -5304
mov     ax,3499           ;AX = 3499
cwd                       ;DX:AX = 3499
        .
        .
```

The AAA Instruction

The **AAA** (**a**djust **a**fter **a**ddition) instruction adjusts the sum of a previous addition operation to a decimal digit (0 to 9). The **AAA** instruction requires the result of the previous addition operation to be placed in **AL**. If the sum was greater 9, register **AH** is incremented and the **carry** and **auxiliary carry** flags are set. If the sum did not overflow, the **AAA** instruction clears both carry flags. The following example defines the syntax for the **AAA** instruction:

```
aaa
```

The following example shows some assembly language statements that use the **AAA** instruction:

```
        .
        .
mov     al,2      ;AL = 2
add     al,8      ;AL = Unconverted result
aaa               ;Convert the result
        .
        .
```

The AAS Instruction

The **AAS** (**a**djust **a**fter **s**ubtraction) instruction adjusts the result of a previous subtraction operation to a decimal digit (0 to 9). The **AAS** instruction requires the result of the previous subtraction operation to be placed in **AL**. If the result was greater than 9, register **AH** is decremented and the **carry** and **auxiliary carry** flags are set. If the result did not overflow, the **AAS** instruction clears the both carry flags. The following example defines the syntax for the **AAS** instruction:

```
aas
```

The following example shows some assembly language statements that use the **AAS** instruction:

```
        .
        .
mov     al,4    ;AL = 4
sub     al,7    ;AL = Unconverted result
aas             ;Convert the result
        .
        .
```

The AAM Instruction

The **AAM** (**a**djust **a**fter **m**ultiply) instruction converts a binary value less than 100 in **AL** to an unpacked binary-coded decimal number in **AX**. After the conversion, register **AH** holds the most significant digit and register **AL** holds the least significant digit. The following example defines the syntax for the **AAM** instruction:

```
aam
```

The following example shows some assembly language statements that use the **AAM** instruction:

```
        .
        .
a       db      7
        .
        .
mov     al,9    ;AL = 9
mul     a       ;AX = Unconverted result
aam             ;Convert the result
        .
        .
```

The AAD Instruction

The **AAD** (ASCII **a**djust before **d**ivision) instruction converts the unpacked digits in **AH** and **AL** to a binary number in **AX**. The following example defines the syntax for the **AAD** instruction:

```
aad
```

The following example shows some assembly language statements that use the **AAD** instruction:

```
        .
        .
        .
a       db      4
        .
        .
        mov     ah,5     ;AH = Most significant digit
        mov     al,3     ;AL = Least significant digit
        aad              ;AX = Binary value
        div     a        ;Perform the division operation
        .
        .
```

The DAA Instruction

The **DAA** (**d**ecimal **a**djust after **a**ddition) instruction converts the sum of a previous addition operation to a packed binary-coded decimal number. The **DAA** instruction requires the result of the previous operation be placed in **AL**. After the conversion, the most significant nibble of **AL** holds the most significant digit, and the least significant nibble of **AL** holds the least significant digit. If the binary-coded number is greater than 99H, the **carry** and **auxiliary carry** flags are set. Otherwise, the **DAA** instruction clears both carry flags. The following example defines the syntax for the **DAA** instruction:

```
daa
```

The following example shows some assembly language statements that use the **DAA** instruction:

```
        •
        •
        •
a       db      34h     ;BCD 34
        •
        •
        mov     al,43h  ;AL = BCD 43
        add     al,a    ;AL = BCD 43 + BCD 34
        daa             ;Convert the result to BCD
        •
        •
```

The DAS Instruction

The **DAS** (**d**ecimal **a**djust after **s**ubtraction) instruction converts the result of a previous subtraction operation to a packed binary-coded decimal number. The **DAS** instruction requires the result of the previous operation to be placed in **AL**. After the conversion, the most significant nibble in **AL** holds the most significant digit in the binary-coded decimal number, and the least significant nibble in **AL** holds the least significant digit in the binary-coded decimal number. If the binary-coded decimal number is greater than 99H, the **carry** and **auxiliary carry** flags are set. Otherwise, the **DAS** instruction clears both carry flags. The following example defines the syntax for the **DAS** instruction:

```
das
```

The following example shows some assembly language statements that use the **DAS** instruction:

```
        .
        .
a   db      32h       ;BCD 32
        .
        .
    mov     al,56h    ;AL = BCD 56
    sub     al,a      ;AL = BCD 56 - BCD 32
    das               ;Convert the result to BCD
        .
        .
```

The Boolean Instructions

Many types of data require True (1) and False (0) values. As you have previously learned, these True/False data types are called Booleans. The 8088 instruction set has four instructions for handling these Boolean data values.

The NOT Instruction

The **NOT** instruction inverts all of the bits for a specified operand. Any of the operand's 0 bits are changed to 1 and any 1 bits are changed to 0. The following table is a truth table for the **NOT** instruction:

Bit	NOT Bit
1	0
0	1

The following example shows the syntax for the **NOT** instruction:

```
not             operand
Where:
operand             is a Reg8, Reg16, Mem8, or Mem16.
```

The following example shows some assembly language statements that use the **NOT** instruction:

```
        .
        .
a       db      32h
        .
        .
        not     a       ;Inverts a
        not     dx      ;Inverts DX
        not     ah      ;Inverts AH
        .
        .
```

The AND Instruction

The **AND** instruction performs a logical AND on two operands. Each of the operands' bits is compared one at a time. If both bits are equal to 1, the corresponding bit in the destination operand is set to 1. Otherwise, the corresponding bit in the destination operand is set to 0. The following table is a truth table for the **AND** instruction:

X	Y	X AND Y
1	1	1
1	0	0
0	1	0
0	0	0

The following example shows the syntax for the **AND** instruction:

```
and             destination,source
Where:
destination          is a Reg8, Reg16, Mem8, or Mem16 and
                     will hold the result of the operation.
source               is a Reg8, Reg16, Mem8, Mem16, Imm8, or
                     Imm16.
```

Notes:

```
Although both the destination and the source operands can
be registers, only one operand at a time can be a memory
location. Additionally, immediate values are only allowed
for source operands.
```

The following example shows some assembly language statements that use the **AND** instruction:

```
        .
        .
a   db     34h
        .
        .
    mov    al,43h
    and    al,a    ;Perform a logical AND on the
                   ; values
        .
        .
```

The OR Instruction

The **OR** instruction performs a logical OR on two operands. Each of the operands' bits is compared one at a time. If either bit is equal to 1, the corresponding bit in the destination operand is set to 1. Otherwise, the corresponding bit in the destination operand is set to 0. The following table is a truth table for the **OR** instruction:

X	Y	X OR Y
1	1	1
1	0	1
0	1	1
0	0	0

The following example shows the syntax for the **OR** instruction:

```
or              destination,source
```

Where:

destination	is a Reg8, Reg16, Mem8, or Mem16 and will hold the result of the operation.
source	is a Reg8, Reg16, Mem8, Mem16, Imm8, or Imm16.

Notes:

Although both the destination and the source operands can be registers, only one operand at a time can be a memory location. Additionally, immediate values are only allowed for source operands.

The following example shows some assembly language statements that use the **OR** instruction:

```
        .
        .
a       db      55h
        .
        .
        mov     dl,33h
        or      dl,a    ;Perform a logical OR on the values
        .
        .
```

The XOR Instruction

The **XOR** (exclusive **or**) instruction performs a logical exclusive OR on two operands. Each of the operands' bits is compared one at a time. If only one of the two bits is equal to 1, the corresponding bit in the destination operand is set to 1. Otherwise, the corresponding bit in the destination operand is set to 0. The following table is a truth table for the **XOR** instruction:

X	Y	X XOR Y
1	1	0
1	0	1
0	1	1
0	0	0

The following example defines the syntax for the **XOR** instruction:

```
xor          destination,source
```
Where:

destination   is a Reg8, Reg16, Mem8, or Mem16 and
                     will hold the result of the operation.

source   is a Reg8, Reg16, Mem8, Mem16, Imm8, or
                     Imm16.

Notes:

Although both the destination and the source operands can be registers, only one operand at a time can be a memory location. Additionally, immediate values are only allowed for source operands.

The following example shows some assembly language statements that use the **XOR** instruction:

```
        .
        .
a    db    23h
        .
        .
     mov    bl,0ffh
     xor    bl,a    ;Perform a logical XOR on the values
        .
        .
```

The Rotate and Shift Instructions

Besides being able to perform logical operations on the bits of a data value, you have a wide variety of assembly language instructions at your disposal for rotating and shifting bits. Not only do the 8088 rotate and shift instructions effect data values, they also greatly effect the **carry** flag.

The ROL Instruction

The **ROL** (**rotate left**) instruction rotates an operand's bits to the left for a specified number of times. During the rotation, the most significant bit is shifted into the **carry** flag and into the operand's least significant bit. The count can either be an immediate value of 1 or is specified in register **CL**. The following example illustrates how the **ROL** instruction rotates a byte value.

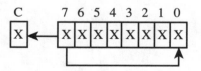

The following example defines the syntax for the **ROL** instruction:

```
rol              operand,count
Where:
operand                 is the value to be rotated and is a
                        Reg8, Reg16, Mem8, or Meg16.
count                   is the number of times to shift the
                        operand and is either an immediate
                        value of 1 or register CL.
```

The following example shows some assembly language statements that use the **ROL** instruction:

```
         .
         .
         .
a    db      0f3h
         .
         .
     rol     a,1       ;Rotate a once to the left
     mov     al,55h
     mov     cl,4
     rol     al,cl     ;Rotate AL four times to the left
         .
         .
```

The ROR Instruction

The **ROR** (**r**otate **r**ight) instruction rotates the bits of an operand to the right for a specified number of times. During the rotation, the least significant bit is rotated into the **carry** flag and into the operand's most significant bit. The count can either be an immediate value of 1 or is specified in register **CL**. The following example illustrates how the **ROR** instruction rotates a byte value:

The following example defines the syntax for the **ROR** instruction:

```
ror              operand,count
Where:
operand          is the value to be rotated and is a
                 Reg8, Reg16, Mem8, or Mem16.
count            is the number of times to shift the
                 operand and is either an immediate
                 value of 1 or is specified in register
                 CL.
```

The following example shows some assembly language statements that use the **ROR** instruction:

```
         .
         .
         .
a    db      0f3h
         .
         .
     ror     a,1      ;Rotate a once to the right
     mov     al,55h
     mov     cl,4
     ror     al,cl    ;Rotate AL four times to the right
         .
         .
```

The RCL Instruction

The **RCL** (rotate carry left) instruction rotates the bits of an operand to the left for a specified number of times. During the rotation, the operand's most significant bit is rotated into the **carry** flag and the **carry** flag's contents are rotated into the operand's least significant bit. The count can either be an immediate value of 1 or is specified in register **CL**. The following example illustrates how the **RCL** rotates a byte value:

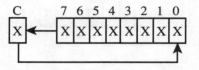

The following example defines the syntax for the **RCL** instruction:

```
rcl              operand,count
Where:
operand          is the value to be rotated and is a
                 Reg8, Reg16, Mem8, or Mem16.
count            is the number of times to shift the
                 operand and is either an immediate
                 value of 1 or is specified in register
                 CL.
```

The following example shows some assembly language statements that use the **RCL** Instruction:

```
         .
         .
a   db   0edh
         .
         .
    rcl  a,1      ;Rotate a once to the left
    mov  al,34h
    mov  cl,3
    rcl  al,cl    ;Rotate AL three times to the left
         .
         .
```

The RCR Instruction

The **RCR** (**r**otate **c**arry **r**ight) instruction rotates the bits of an operand to the right for a specified number of times. During the rotation, the operand's least significant bit is rotated into the **carry** flag and the **carry** flag is rotated into the operand's most significant bit. The count can either be an immediate value of 1 or is specified in register **CL**. The following example illustrates how the **RCR** instruction rotates a byte value:

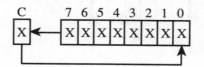

The following example defines the syntax for the **RCR** instruction:

```
rcr          operand,count
Where:
operand              is the value to be rotated and is a
                     Reg8, Reg16, Mem8, or Mem16.
count                is the number of times to shift the
                     operand and is either an immediate
                     value of 1 or is specified in register
                     CL.
```

The following example shows some assembly language statements that use the **RCR** instruction:

```
        .
        .
a    dw      0f34dh
        .
        .
     rcr     a,1        ;Rotate a once to the right
     mov     dx,5567h
     mov     cl,5
     rcr     dx,cl      ;Rotate DX five times to the right
        .
```

The SAL Instruction

The **SAL** (shift arithmetic left) instruction shifts the bits of an operand to the left for a specified number of times. During the shift, a 0 is shifted into the operand's least significant bit and the operand's most significant bit is shifted into the **carry** flag. The number of shifts can either be an immediate value of 1 or can be specified in register **CL**. The following example illustrates how the **SAL** instruction shifts a byte value:

The following example defines the syntax for the **SAL** instruction:

```
sal             operand, count
Where:
operand                 is the value to be shifted and is a
                        Reg8, Reg16, Mem8, or Mem16.
count                   is the number of times to shift the
                        operand and is either an immediate
                        value of 1 or is specified in register
                        CL.
```

The following example shows some assembly language statements that use the **SAL** instruction:

```
        .
        .
a    dw      034feh
        .
        .
     sal     a,1                     ;Shift a once to the left
     mov     dx,45cbh
     mov     cl,4
     sal     dx,cl                   ;Shift DX four times
        .
        .
```

The SAR Instruction

The **SAR** (shift **a**rithmetic **r**ight) instruction shifts the bits of an operand to the right for a specified number of times. During the shift, the operand's sign bit (most significant bit) is preserved and the operand's least significant bit is shifted into the **carry** flag. The number of shifts can either be an immediate value of 1 or specified in register **CL**. The following example illustrates how the **SAR** instruction shifts a byte value:

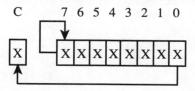

The following example defines the syntax for the **SAR** instruction:

```
sar             operand,count
Where:
operand         is the value to be shifted and is a
                Reg8, Reg16, Mem8, or Mem16.
count           is the number of times to shift the
                operand and is either an immediate
                value of 1 or is specified in register
                CL.
```

The following example shows some assembly language statements that use the **SAR** instruction:

```
        .
        .
a    db     45
        .
        .
     sar    a,1      ;Shift a once to the right
     mov    ch,35h
     mov    cl,2
     sar    ch,cl    ;Shift CH two times
        .
        .
```

The SHL Instruction

The **SHL** (**shift left**) instruction shifts the bits of an operand to the left for a specified number of times. During the shift, a 0 is shifted into the operand's least significant bit and the operand's most significant bit is shifted into the **carry** flag. Note that this is the same operation that the **SAL** instruction performs. The number of shifts can either be an immediate value of 1 or can be specified in register **CL**. The following example illustrates how the **SHL** instruction shifts a byte value:

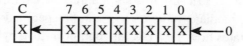

The following example defines the syntax for the **SHL** instruction:

```
shl             operand,count
Where:
operand         is the value to be shifted and is a
                Reg8, Reg16, Mem8, or Mem16.
count           is the number of times to shift the
                operand and is either an immediate
                value of 1 or is specified in register
                CL.
```

The following example shows some assembly language statements that use the **SHL** instruction:

```
        .
        .
a   db      44h
        .
        .
    shl     a,1     ;Shift a once to the left
    mov     bh,33h
    mov     cl,4
    shl     bh,cl   ;Shift BL four times
        .
        .
```

The SHR Instruction

The **SHR** (**sh**ift **r**ight) instruction shifts the bits of an operand to the right for a specified number of times. During the shift, a 0 is shifted into the operand's most significant bit and the operand's least significant bit is shifted into the **carry** flag. The number of shifts can either be an immediate value of 1 or can be specified in register **CL**. The following example illustrates how the **SHR** instruction shifts a byte value:

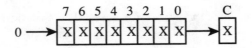

The following example defines the syntax for **SHR**:

```
shr          operand,count
Where:
operand               is the value to be shifted and is a
                      Reg8, Reg16, Mem8, or Mem16.

count                 is the number of times to shift the
                      operand and is either an immediate
                      value or 1 or is specified in register
                      CL.
```

The following example shows some assembly language statements that use the **SHR** instruction:

```
        .
        .
        .
a       db      45
        .
        .
        shr     a,1      ;Shift a once to the right
        mov     ch,35h
        mov     cl,2
        shr     ch,cl    ;Shift CH two times
        .
        .
```

The Comparison Instructions

As with all other programming languages, assembly language programs are often required to perform different operations depending on the value of a piece of data. The 8088 has two instructions for performing comparisons: **CMP** and **TEST**.

The CMP Instruction

The **CMP** (**comp**are) instruction compares the value of two operands. Essentially, the **CMP** instruction subtracts the two operands. However, the destination operand is unaffected by the operation. After comparing the two operands, the 8088 sets the processor flags accordingly. Once the flags have been set to indicate the result of the comparison, the flags can be used by the 8088 jump instructions (more about those in a bit) to alter the direction of program execution. The following example defines the syntax for the **CMP** instruction:

```
cmp               destination,source
Where:
destination       is a Reg8, Reg16, Mem8, or Mem16.
source            is a Reg8, Reg16, Mem8, Mem16, Imm8, or
                  Imm16.
```

Notes:

```
Although both the destination and the source operands can
be registers, only one operand at a time can be a memory
location. Additionally, immediate values are only allowed
for source operands.
```

115

The following example shows some assembly language statements that use the **CMP** instruction:

```
        .
        .
a       db      34
        .
        .
        mov     ah,53
        cmp     ah,a    ;Compare the two values
        .
        .
```

The TEST Instruction

The **TEST** instruction performs a logical AND on two operands. Unlike the **AND** instruction, the **TEST** instruction only sets the 8088's flags and does not effect the destination operand. Once the flags have been set to indicate the result of the operation, the 8088 can use the flags to jump instructions to alter the direction of program execution. The following example defines the syntax for the **TEST** instruction:

```
test            destination,source
Where:
destination     is a Reg8, Reg16, Mem8, or Mem16.
source          is a Reg8, Reg16, Mem8, Mem16, Imm8, or
                Imm16.

Notes:

Although both the destination and source operands can be
registers, only one operand at a time can be a memory
location. Additionally, immediate values are only allowed
for source operands.
```

The following example shows an assembly language statement that uses the **TEST** instruction:

```
        .
        .
a    db     4FH
        .
        .
     mov    al,33h
     test   al,a      ;AND the two values
        .
        .
```

The Jump Instructions

Like programs written in other programming languages, assembly language programs do not always execute straight from the top to the bottom. Almost all programs take detours along the way. To provide for these detours, the 8088 has a wide variety of jump instructions. These jump instructions can cause program execution to follow another path either unconditionally or conditionally.

The JMP Instruction

The **JMP** (**jump**) instruction moves program execution to any location within the computer memory. The following example defines the syntax for the **JMP** instruction:

```
jmp           operand
Where:
operand             is a label, Reg16, or Mem16.
```

The following example shows some assembly language statements that use the **JMP** instruction:

```
            .
            .
        jmp    next      ;Jump to the memory location with
                         ; the label "next"
            .
            .
            .
next:       .
            .
            .
```

The JA Instruction

The **JA** (**j**ump if **a**bove) instruction transfers program execution to a specified location if the first operand in an unsigned comparison is greater than the second operand. The **JA** instruction performs the same function as the **JNBE** instruction. The following example defines the syntax for the **JA** instruction:

```
ja            label
```
Where:
```
label                 is a label that is no more than -128 or
                      127 bytes away from the current memory
                      location.
```

The following example shows some assembly language statements that use the **JA** instruction:

```
          .
          .
      cmp    bx,5504    ;Jump if
      ja     next       ; BX > 5504
          .
          .
next:     .
          .
          .
```

The JAE Instruction

The **JAE** (jump if **a**bove or **e**qual) instruction transfers program execution to a specified location if the first operand in an unsigned comparison is above or equal to the second operand. The **JAE** instruction performs the same function as the **JNB** instruction. The following example defines the syntax for the **JAE** instruction:

```
jae          label
Where:
label                is a label that is no more than −128 or
                     127 bytes away from the current memory
                     location.
```

The following example shows some assembly language statements that use **JAE** instruction:

```
          .
          .
      cmp    ax,578     ;Jump if
      jae    next       ; ax >= 578
          .
          .
next:     .
          .
```

The JB Instruction

The **JB** (jump if **b**elow) instruction transfers program execution to a specified location if the first operand in an unsigned comparison is less than the second operand. The **JB** instruction performs the same function as the **JNAE** instruction. The following example defines the syntax for the **JB** instruction:

```
jb              label
Where:
label                   is a label that is no more than -128 or
                        127 bytes away from the current memory
                        location.
```

The following example shows some assembly language statements that use the **JB** instruction:

```
        .
        .
        cmp     al,55       ;Jump if AL
        jb      next        ; is < 55
        .
        .
next:   .
        .
        .
```

The JBE Instruction

The **JBE** (jump if **b**elow or **e**qual) instruction transfers program execution to a specified location if the first operand in an unsigned comparison is below or equal to the second operand. The **JBE** instruction performs the same function as the **JNA** instruction. The following example defines the syntax for the **JBE** instruction:

```
jbe             label
Where:
label                   is a label that is no more than -128 or
                        127 bytes away from the current memory
                        location.
```

The following example shows some assembly language statements that use the **JBE** instruction:

```
        .
        .
        .
        cmp    bl,55h    ;Jump if
        jbe    next      ; bl <= 55h
        .
        .
next:   .
        .
        .
```

The JC Instruction

The **JC** (jump **c**arry) instruction transfers program execution to a specified location if the **carry** flag is set. The following example defines the syntax for the **JC** instruction:

```
jc            label
```

Where:

```
label              is a label that is no more than -128 or
                   127 bytes away from the current memory
                   location.
```

The following example shows some assembly language statements that use the **JC** instruction:

```
        .
        .
        .
        sub    al,55
        jc     next      ;Jump if AL - 55 set the carry
                         ; flag
        .
        .
next:   .
        .
        .
```

The JE Instruction

The **JE** (**j**ump if **e**qual) instruction transfers program execution to a specified location if both operands in a comparison are equal. The following example defines the syntax for the **JE** instruction:

```
je          label
Where:
label                is a label that is no more than -128 or
                     127 bytes away from the current memory
                     location.
```

The following example shows some assembly language statements that use the **JE** instruction:

```
        .
        .
        cmp  bx,445    ;Jump if
        je   next      ; BX = 445
        .
        .
next:   .
        .
        .
```

The JG Instruction

The **JG** (**j**ump if **g**reater) instruction transfers program execution to a specified location if the first operand in a signed comparison is greater than the second operand. The **JG** instruction performs the same function as the **JNLE** instruction. The following example defines the syntax for the **JG** instruction:

```
jg          label
Where:
label                is a label that is no more than -128 or
                     127 bytes away from the current memory
                     location.
```

The following example shows some assembly language statements that use the **JG** instruction:

```
            .
            .
       cmp  al,-101    ;Jump if
       jg   next       ; AL > -101
            .
            .
next:       .
            .
            .
```

The JGE Instruction

The **JGE** (**j**ump if **g**reater or **e**qual) instruction transfers program execution to a specified location if the first operand in a signed comparison is greater than or equal to the second operand. The **JGE** instruction performs the same instruction as the **JNL** instruction. The following example defines the syntax for the **JGE** instruction:

```
jge            label
Where:
label                  is a label that is no more than -128 or
                       127 bytes away from the current memory
                       location.
```

The following example shows some assembly language statements that use the **JGE** instruction:

```
            .
            .
       cmp  bl,67      ;Jump if
       jge  next       ; BL >= 67
            .
            .
next:       .
            .
            .
```

The JL Instruction

The **JL** (**jump if less**) instruction transfers program execution to a specified location if the first operand in a signed comparison is less than the second operand. The **JL** instruction performs the same function as the **JNGE** instruction. The following example defines the syntax for the **JL** instruction:

```
jl            label
Where:
label                     is a label that is no more than -128 or
                          127 bytes away from the current memory
                          location.
```

The following example shows some assembly language statements that use the **JL** instruction:

```
        .
        .
        cmp   dx,-455   ;Jump if
        jl    next      ; dx < -455
        .
        .
next:   .
        .
        .
```

The JLE Instruction

The **JLE** (**jump if less or equal**) instruction transfers program execution to a specified location if the first operand in a signed comparison is less than or equal to the second operand. The **JLE** instruction performs the same function as the **JNG** instruction. The following example defines the syntax for the **JLE** instruction:

```
jle           label
Where:
label                     is a label that is no more than -128 or
                          127 bytes away from the current memory
                          location.
```

The following example shows some assembly language statements that use the **JLE** instruction:

```
        .
        .
        cmp    ax,-9999  ;Jump if
        jle    next      ; AX <= -9999
        .
        .
next:   .
        .
        .
```

The JNA Instruction

The **JNA** (**j**ump if **n**ot **a**bove) instruction transfers program execution to a specified location if the first operand in an unsigned comparison is not above the second operand. The **JNA** instruction performs the same function as the **JBE** instruction. The following example defines the syntax for the **JNA** instruction:

```
jna          label
Where:
label                 is a label that is no more than -128 or
                      127 bytes away from the current memory
                      location.
```

The following example shows some assembly language statements that use the **JNA** instruction:

```
        .
        .
        cmp    bl,55h    ;Jump if
        jna    next      ; bl <= 55h
        .
        .
next:   .
        .
        .
```

The JNAE Instruction

The **JNAE** (jump if **n**ot **a**bove or **e**qual) instruction transfers program execution to a specified location if the first operand in an unsigned comparison is not above or equal to the second operand. The **JNAE** instruction performs the same function as the **JB** instruction. The following example defines the syntax for the **JNAE** instruction:

```
jnae          label
Where:
label                   is a label that is no more than -128 or
                        127 bytes away from the current memory
                        location.
```

The following example shows some assembly language statements that use the **JNAE** instruction:

```
        .
        .
        .
        cmp    al,55       ;Jump if AL
        jnae   next        ; is < 55
        .
        .
next:   .
        .
        .
```

The JNB Instruction

The **JNB** (jump if **n**ot **b**elow) instruction transfers program execution to a specified location if the first operand in an unsigned comparison is not below the second operand. The **JNB** instruction performs the same function as the **JAE** instruction. The following example defines the syntax for the **JNB** instruction:

```
jnb           label
Where:
label                   is a label that is no more than -128 or
                        127 bytes away from the current memory
                        location.
```

The following example shows some assembly language statements that use the **JNB** instruction:

```
            .
            .
     cmp    ax,578      ;Jump if
     jnb    next        ; ax >= 578
            .
            .
next:       .
            .
            .
```

The JNBE Instruction

The **JNBE** (jump if **n**ot **b**elow or **e**qual) instruction transfers program execution to a specified location if the first operand in an unsigned comparison is not below or equal to the second operand. The **JNBE** instruction performs the same function as the **JA** instruction. The following example defines the syntax for the **JNBE** instruction:

jnbe   label

Where:

label   is a label that is no more than -128 or
                       127 bytes away from the current memory
                       location.

The following example shows some assembly language statements that use the **JNBE** instruction:

```
            .
            .
     cmp    bx,5504     ;Jump if
     jnbe   next        ; BX > 5504
            .
            .
next:       .
            .
            .
```

127

The JNC Instruction

The **JNC** (**j**ump if **n**ot **c**arry) instruction transfers program execution to a specified location if the **carry** flag is not set. The following example defines the syntax for the **JNC** instruction:

```
jnc             label
Where:
label                   is a label that is no more than -128 or
                        127 bytes away from the current memory
                        location.
```

The following example shows some assembly language statements that use the **JNC** instruction:

```
        .
        .
        sub   al,55
        jnc   next       ;Jump if AL - 55 didn't set the
                         ; carry flag
        .
        .
next:   .
        .
        .
```

The JNE Instruction

The **JNE** (**j**ump if **n**ot **e**qual) instruction transfers program execution to a specified location if the first operand in a comparison is not equal to the second operand. The **JNE** instruction performs the same function as the **JNZ** instruction. The following example defines the syntax for the **JNE** instruction:

```
jne             label
Where:
label                   is a label that is no more than -128 or
                        127 bytes away from the current memory
                        location.
```

The following example shows some assembly language statements that use the **JNE** instruction:

```
            .
            .
            .
        cmp   al,54      ;Jump if
        jne   next       ; AL <> 54
            .
            .
next:       .
            .
            .
```

The JNG Instruction

The **JNG** (jump if **n**ot **g**reater) instruction transfers program execution to a specified location if the first operand in a signed comparison is not greater than the second operand. The **JNG** instruction performs the same function as the **JLE** instruction. The following example defines the syntax for the **JNG** instruction:

```
jng           label
Where:
label                   is a label that is no more than -128 or
                        127 bytes away from the current memory
                        location.
```

The following example shows some of assembly language statements that use the **JNG** instruction:

```
            .
            .
        cmp   ax,-9999  ;Jump if
        jng   next      ; AX <= -9999
            .
            .
next:       .
            .
            .
```

The JNGE Instruction

The **JNGE** (jump if **n**ot **g**reater or **e**qual) instruction transfers program execution to a specified location if the first operand in a signed comparison is not greater than or equal to the second operand. The **JNGE** instruction performs the same function as the **JL** instruction. The following example defines the syntax for the **JNGE** instruction:

```
jnge          label
Where:
label                   is a label that is no more than -128 or
                        127 bytes away from the current memory
                        location.
```

The following example shows some assembly language statements that use the **JNGE** instruction:

```
          .
          .
          .
          cmp    dx,-455    ;Jump if
          jnge   next       ; dx < -455
          .
          .
next:     .
          .
          .
```

The JNL Instruction

The **JNL** (jump if **n**ot **l**ess) instruction transfers program execution to a specified location if the first operand in a signed comparison is not less than the second operand. The **JNL** instruction performs the same function as the **JGE** instruction. The following example defines the syntax for the **JNL** instruction:

```
jnl           label
Where:
label                   is a label that is no more than -128 or
                        127 bytes away from the current memory
                        location.
```

The following example shows some assembly language statements that use the **JNL** instruction:

```
        .
        .
        cmp   bl,67      ;Jump if
        jnl   next       ; BL >= 67
        .
        .
next:   .
        .
        .
```

The JNLE Instruction

The **JNLE** (jump if **n**ot **l**ess or **e**qual) instruction transfers program execution to a specified location if the first operand in a signed comparison is not less than or equal to the second operand. The **JNLE** instruction performs the same function as the **JG** instruction. The following example defines the syntax for the **JNLE** instruction:

```
jnle          label
Where:
label                   is a label that is no more than -128 or
                        127 bytes away from the current memory
                        location.
```

The following example shows some assembly language statements that use the **JNLE** instruction:

```
        .
        .
        cmp   al,-101    ;Jump if
        jnle  next       ; AL > -101
        .
        .
next:   .
        .
        .
```

The JNO Instruction

The **JNO** (jump if **n**ot **o**verflow) instruction transfers program execution to a specified memory location if the **overflow** flag is not set. The following example defines the syntax for the **JNO** instruction:

```
jno             label
Where:
label                   is a label that is no more than -128 or
                        127 bytes away from the current memory
                        location.
```

The following example shows some assembly language statements that use the **JNO** instruction:

```
        .
        .
        add     al,245      ;Jump if
        jno     next        ; AL + 245 didn't overflow
        .
        .
next:   .
        .
        .
```

The JNP Instruction

The **JNP** (jump if **n**o **p**arity) instruction transfers program execution to a specified memory location if the result of a previous instruction does not have parity. The **JNP** instruction performs the same function as the **JPO** instruction. The following example defines the syntax for the **JNP** instruction:

```
jnp             label
Where:
label                   is a label that is no more than -128 or
                        127 bytes away from the current memory
                        location.
```

The following example shows some assembly language statements that use the **JNP** instruction:

```
        .
        .
        and   al,al     ;Jump if AL
        jnp   next      ; doesn't have parity
        .
        .
next:   .
        .
        .
```

The JNS Instruction

The **JNS** (**j**ump if **n**o **s**ign) instruction transfers program execution to a specified memory location if the result of a previous instruction did not set the **sign** flag. The following example defines the syntax for the **JNS** instruction:

```
jns           label
```

Where:

label   is a label that is no more than –128 or
                     127 bytes away from the current memory
                     location.

The following example shows some assembly language statements that use the **JNS** instruction:

```
        .
        .
        and   dx,dx     ;Jump if
        jns   next      ; DX is positive
        .
        .
next:   .
        .
        .
```

The JNZ Instruction

The **JNZ** (**jump if not zero**) instruction transfers program execution to a specified memory location if the result of a previous instruction did not set the **zero** flag. The **JNZ** instruction performs the same function as the **JNE** instruction. The following example defines the syntax for the **JNZ** instruction:

```
jnz             label
Where:
label                   is a label that is no more than -128 or
                        127 bytes away from the current memory
                        location.
```

The following example shows some assembly language statements that use the **JNZ** instruction:

```
        .
        .
        .
        or      bx,bx       ;Jump if
        jnz     next        ; BX <> 0
        .
        .
next:   .
        .
        .
```

The JS Instruction

The **JS** (**jump if sign**) instruction transfers program execution to a specified memory location if the result of a previous instruction set the **sign** flag. The following example defines the syntax for the **JS** instruction:

```
js              label
Where:
label                   is a label that is no more than -128 or
                        127 bytes away from the current memory
                        location.
```

The following example shows some assembly language statements that use the **JS** instruction:

```
        .
        .
        and    ax,ax      ;Jump if
        js     next       ; AX is negative
        .
        .
next:   .
        .
        .
```

The JO Instruction

The **JO** (jump if overflow) instruction transfers program execution to a specified memory location if the result of a previous instruction set the overflow flag. The following example defines the syntax for the **JO** instruction:

```
jo             label
```
Where:

```
label                  is a label that is no more than -128 or
                       127 bytes away from the current memory
                       location.
```

The following example shows some assembly language statements that use the **JO** instruction:

```
        .
        .
        add    ax,55678   ;Jump if
        jo     next       ; AX + 55678 overflowed
        .
        .
next:   .
        .
        .
```

The JP Instruction

The **JP** (**j**ump if **p**arity) instruction transfers program execution to a specified memory location if the result of a previous instruction had parity. The **JP** instruction performs the same function as the **JPE** instruction. The following example defines the syntax for the **JP** instruction:

```
jp              label
Where:
label                    is a label that is no more than -128 or
                         127 bytes away from the current memory
                         location.
```

The following example shows some assembly language statements that use the **JP** instruction:

```
        .
        .
        .
        and    ax,ax        ;Jump if AX
        jp     next         ; has parity
        .
        .
        .
next:   .
        .
        .
```

The JPE Instruction

The **JPE** (**j**ump if **p**arity **e**ven) instruction transfers program execution to a specified memory location if the result of a previous instruction had even parity. The **JPE** instruction performs the same function as the **JP** instruction. The following example defines the syntax for the **JPE** instruction:

```
jpe             label
Where:
label                    is a label that is no more than -128 or
                         127 bytes away from the current memory
                         location.
```

The following example shows some assembly language statements that use the **JPE** instruction:

```
            .
            .
       and   ax,ax     ;Jump if AX
       jpe   next      ; has even parity
            .
            .
next:       .
            .
            .
```

The JPO Instruction

The **JPO** (jump if **p**arity **o**dd) instruction transfers program execution to a specified memory location if the result of a previous instruction had odd parity. The **JPO** instruction performs the same function as the **JNP** instruction. The following example defines the syntax for the **JPO** instruction:

jpo   label

Where:

label   is a label that is no more than −128 or
                         127 bytes away from the current memory
                         location.

The following example shows some assembly language statements that use the **JPO** instruction:

```
            .
            .
       and   al,al     ;Jump if AL
       jpo   next      ; had odd parity
            .
            .
next:       .
            .
            .
```

The JCXZ Instruction

The **JCXZ** (jump if **CX** is zero) instruction transfers program execution to a specified memory location if register **CX** is equal to zero. The following example defines the syntax for the **JCXZ** instruction:

```
jcxz            label
Where:
label                   is a label that is no more than −128 or
                        127 bytes away from the current memory
                        location.
```

The following example shows some assembly language statements that use the **JCXZ** instruction:

```
            .
            .
next:       .
            .
            .
            dec   cx          ;Decrement CX
            jcxz  next        ;Jump if CX = 0
            .
            .
```

The Iteration Instructions

Although you can use the 8088's jump instructions to implement loops within programs, there are 8088 instructions that are made just for implementing loops. These loop instructions can transfer program execution both conditionally and unconditionally.

The LOOP Instruction

The **LOOP** instruction loops repeatedly to a specified memory location. Each time the **LOOP** instruction is executed, the **CX** register is decremented and if the result is not equal to 0, program execution is transferred to a specified memory location. The following example defines the syntax for the **LOOP** instruction:

```
loop           label
Where:
label                      is a label that is no more than -128 or
                           127 bytes away from the current memory
                           location.
```

The following example shows some assembly language statements that use the **LOOP** instruction:

```
          .
          .
next:     .
          .
          .
          loop   next       ;Loop until CX = 0
          .
          .
```

The LOOPE Instruction

The **LOOPE** (**loop** if **equal**) instruction loops repeatedly to a specified memory location if the result of a previous comparison set the **zero** flag and the **CX** register is not equal to 0. As with the **LOOP** instruction, the **CX** register is decremented each time the

LOOPE instruction is executed. The **LOOPE** instruction performs the same function as the **LOOPZ** instruction. The following example defines the syntax for the **LOOPE** instruction:

```
loope        label
Where:
label                   is a label that is no more than -128 or
                        127 bytes away from the current memory
                        location.
```

The following example shows some assembly language statements that use the **LOOPE** instruction:

```
              .
              .
next:         .
              .
        cmp   ax,55      ;Loop while AX = 55
        loope next      ; and CX <> 0
              .
              .
```

The LOOPNE Instruction

The **LOOPNE** (**loop** if **n**ot **e**qual) instruction loops repeatedly to a specified memory location if the result of a previous comparison did not set the **zero** flag and the **CX** register is not equal to 0. As with the **LOOP** instruction, the **CX** register is decremented each time the **LOOPNE** instruction is executed. The **LOOPNE** instruction performs the same function as the **LOOPNZ** instruction. The following example defines the syntax for the **LOOPNE** instruction:

```
loopne       label
Where:
label                   is a label that is no more than -128 or
                        127 bytes away from the current memory
                        location.
```

The following example shows some assembly language statements that use the **LOOPNE** instruction:

```
                 .
                 .
next:            .
                 .
                 .
         cmp     ax,55     ;Loop while AX <> 55
         loopne  next      ; and CX <> 0
                 .
                 .
```

The LOOPNZ Instruction

The **LOOPNZ** (**loop** if **not** **zero**) instruction loops repeatedly to a specified memory location if the **zero** flag is not set and the **CX** register is not equal to 0. As with the **LOOP** instruction, the **CX** register is decremented each time the **LOOPNZ** instruction is executed. The **LOOPNZ** instruction performs the same function as the **LOOPNE** instruction. The following example defines the syntax for the **LOOPNZ** instruction:

```
loopnz        label
Where:
label                 is a label that is no more than -128 or
                      127 bytes away from the current memory
                      location.
```

The following example shows some assembly language statements that use the **LOOPNZ** instruction:

```
            .
            .
            .
next:       .
            .
            .
      or      al,al    ;Loop while AL <> 0
      loopnz  next     ; and CX <> 0
            .
            .
```

The LOOPZ Instruction

The **LOOPZ** (**loop** if zero) instruction loops repeatedly to a specified memory location if the result of an instruction sets the **zero** flag and the **CX** register is not equal to 0. As with the **LOOP** instruction, the **CX** register is decremented each time the **LOOPZ** instruction is executed. The **LOOPZ** instruction performs the same function as the **LOOPE** instruction. The following example defines the syntax for the **LOOPZ** instruction:

```
loopz         label
Where:
label                is a label that is no more than -128 or
                     127 bytes away from the current memory
                     location.
```

The following example shows some assembly language statements that use the **LOOPZ** instruction:

```
            .
            .
next:.
            .
            .
        and     ax,ax    ;Loop while AX = 0
        loop    next     ; and CX <> 0
            .
            .
```

The Miscellaneous Instructions

In addition to all of the instructions covered so far, the 8088 has a variety of instructions for performing a number of useful tasks. These miscellaneous instructions perform such tasks as setting flags, clearing flags, inverting flags, and not doing anything at all.

The CLC Instruction

The **CLC** (**c**lear **c**arry flag) instruction clears the **carry** flag by setting it to 0. The following example defines the syntax for the **CLC** instruction:

```
    clc
```

The following example shows an assembly language statement that uses the **CLC** instruction:

```
        .
        .
        clc     ;Clear the carry flag
        .
        .
```

The CLD Instruction

The **CLD** (**cl**ear **d**irection flag) clears the direction flag by setting it to 0. The following example defines the syntax for the **CLD** instruction:

```
cld
```

The following example shows an assembly language statement that uses the **CLD** instruction:

```
        .
        .
        cld     ;Clear the direction flag
        .
        .
```

The CLI Instruction

The **CLI** (**cl**ear **i**nterrupt flag) clears the interrupt flag by setting it to 0. When the interrupt flag is cleared, all maskable interrupts are disabled. The following example defines the syntax for the **CLI** instruction:

```
cli
```

The following example shows an assembly language statement that uses the **CLI** instruction:

```
        .
        .
        cli     ;Disable the interrupts
        .
        .
```

The CMC Instruction

The **CMC** (**c**omplement **c**arry flag) instruction inverts the value of the **carry** flag. The following example defines the syntax for the **CMC** instruction:

```
cmc
```

The following example shows an assembly language statement that uses the **CMC** instruction:

```
        .
        .
    cmc     ;Invert the carry flag
        .
        .
```

The LAHF Instruction

The **LAHF** (load **AH** from **f**lags) instruction loads

- bit 0 of register **AH** with the **carry** flag

- bit 2 of register **AH** with the **parity** flag

- bit 4 of register **AH** with the **auxiliary carry** flag

- bit 6 of register **AH** with the **zero** flag

- bit 7 of register **AH** with the **sign** flag.

The following example defines the syntax for the **LAHF** instruction:

```
    lahf
```

The following example shows an assembly language statement that uses the **LAHF** instruction:

```
        .
        .
    lahf    ;Load AH with the flags
        .
        .
```

The NOP Instruction

The **NOP** (**no op**eration) instruction does not have a function. It is often used to make a memory location addressable. The following example defines the syntax for the **NOP** instruction:

```
nop
```

The following example shows an assembly language statement that uses the **NOP** instruction:

```
            .
            .
next:       nop
            .
            .
```

The SAHF Instruction

The **SAHF** (store **AH** in flags) instruction loads

- bit 0 of register **AH** into the **carry** flag

- bit 2 of register **AH** into the **parity** flag

- bit 4 of register **AH** into the **auxiliary carry** flag

- bit 6 of register **AH** into the **zero** flag

- bit 7 of register **AH** into the **sign** flag.

The following example defines the syntax for the **SAHF** instruction:

```
sahf
```

The following example shows an assembly language statement that uses the **SAHF** instruction:

```
        .
        .
        sahf    ;Store AH in the flags
        .
        .
```

The STC Instruction

The **STC** (**set c**arry flag) instruction sets the **carry** flag by setting it to 1. The following example defines the syntax for the **STC** instruction:

```
stc
```

The following example shows an assembly language statement that uses the **STC** instruction:

```
        .
        .
        stc     ;Set the carry flag
        .
        .
```

The STD Instruction

The **STD** (**set d**irection flag) instruction sets the **direction** flag by setting it to 1. The following example defines the syntax for the **STD** instruction:

```
std
```

The following example shows an assembly language instruction that uses the **STD** instruction:

```
        .
        .
std     ;Set the direction flag
        .
        .
```

The STI Instruction

The **STI** (**set** interrupt flag) instruction sets the **interrupt** flag by setting it to 1. When the **interrupt** flag is set, all maskable interrupts are enabled. The following example defines the syntax for the **STI** instruction:

```
sti
```

The following example shows an assembly language instruction that uses the **STI** instruction:

```
        .
        .
sti     ;Enable the interrupts
        .
        .
```

Summary

This chapter introduced you to a wide variety of 8088 assembly language instructions. These instructions perform diverse operations, such as storing data in and retrieving data from registers and memory, arithmetic calculations, unconditional and conditional transfers of program execution, manipulating the flags, and more. Although these are the bulk of the instructions for the 8088 microprocessor, future chapters will teach you a number of other instructions that you need to write effective assembly language programs.

Chapter 6

Addressing Modes

T he 8088 microprocessor uses four basic addressing modes to access as wide a variety of data as possible: the immediate addressing mode, the register addressing mode, the direct addressing mode, and the indirect addressing mode.

This chapter teaches you

- what each of the four addressing modes are

- how you use the four addressing modes in an 8088 assembly language program.

The Immediate Addressing Mode

The immediate addressing mode uses immediate operands to reference data. An immediate operand is any numeric constant that is known at assembly time. You can use immediate operands with many of the instructions for the 8088. However, you can never use an immediate operand as the destination operand for an instruction that requires both a source and destination operand. This is a logical restriction. The destination operand of an instruction is where the instruction is supposed to store the result of an operation. Consequently, it would be illogical to assign a new value to a constant. The following example shows some assembly language statements that use the immediate addressing mode:

```
        .
        .
cr   equ    13        ;Define a carriage return constant
        .
        .
     mov    al,55   ;Loads AL with immediate value 55
     xor    bx,33h  ;XORs AX with immediate value 33h
     mov    ah,cr   ;Loads AH with immediate value cr
     sub    cx,6678 ;Subtract immediate value 6678
                    ; from CX
        .
        .
```

The Register Addressing Mode

The register addressing mode uses register operands to reference data. The register addressing mode is more properly called the register-direct addressing mode because the referenced data is the value that the register holds at the time the instruction is executed. Since you can use register operands with just about any of the 8088's instructions, the register addressing mode is probably the most widely used of the 8088's addressing modes. The following example shows some assembly language statements that use the register addressing mode:

```
              .
              .
array    dw      10 dup (?)
              .
              .
         mov    ax,bx              ;Both operands are regis-
                                   ; ter operands
         sub    al,55              ;The destination is a
                                   ; register operand
         mov    bx                 ;The only operand is a
                                   ; register operand
         mov    array,ax           ;The source is a register
                                   ; operand
              .
              .
```

The Direct Memory Addressing Mode

The direct memory addressing mode uses direct memory operands to reference data. A direct memory operand is any offset address that can be calculated at assembly time. Unless it is overridden with the segment-override operator, the **DS** segment register calculates the actual location of a direct memory address in the computer memory. The following example shows some assembly language statements that use the direct memory addressing mode:

```
        .
        .
value   dw      100h
        .

        .
        mov     bx,value        ;Use direct memory
                                ; addressing to load BX with
                                ; 100h
        mov     value,34        ;Use direct memory
                                ; addressing to save a new
                                ; value

        .
        .
```

In addition to using labels to represent direct memory addresses, you can use numeric constants. However, you must specify a segment when using numeric constants. If you do not specify a segment, the assembler incorrectly assumes that the immediate addressing mode is being used. The following example shows some assembly language statements that use numeric constants for the direct memory addressing mode:

```
        .
        .
mov     al,ds:33h               ;Load AL with the value at
                                ; DS:33H
mov     ss:2,ax                 ;Save AX at SS:02H
        .
        .
```

The Indirect Memory Addressing Mode

The indirect addressing mode uses registers to point to data. In the indirect addressing mode, the registers are a lot like pointers in high-level languages. As was stated earlier, the **BX** and **BP** registers are base registers, and the **DI** and **SI** registers are index registers. These four 16-bit registers are the only registers that you can use for indirect memory addressing. With a few exceptions, you can use all four registers similarly.

Types of Indirect Memory Addressing Modes

There are four basic types of indirect memory addressing modes: the register indirect addressing mode, the based or indexed addressing mode, the based indexed addressing mode, and the based indexed with displacement addressing mode.

Register indirect addressing mode

The simplest of the four indirect addressing modes is the register indirect addressing mode. The following example illustrates the syntax for using the register indirect addressing mode:

```
[register]
```
Where:

register   is either register **BX, BP, DI,** or **SI.**

As the previous example shows, the register is surrounded by brackets. These brackets are the index operators. They tell the assembler that the register's value points to another value and is not the value to use in the register direct addressing mode. The following example shows assembly language statements that use the register indirect addressing mode:

```
        .

        .

mov     ax,[dx]     ;Load AX with the value pointed to
                    ; by DI
add     [bx],al     ;Add al to the value pointed to by
                    ; BX

        .

        .
```

Based or indexed addressing mode

Like the register indirect addressing mode, the based or indexed addressing mode provides a pointer to a value and not the actual value itself. The following example illustrates the syntax for using the based or indexed addressing mode:

```
displacement[register]
or
[register + displacement]
```

Where:

```
displacement        is either a constant, a memory address,
                    or both.

register            is either register BX, BP, DI, or SI.
```

The following example shows some assembly language statements that use the based or indexed addressing modes:

```
        .
        .
table       db      100 dup (?)
        .
        .
    mov     al,table[bx]        ;Load AL with the value
                                ; pointed to by table and
                                ; BX
    mov     al,[table + bx]     ;Does the same as the
                                ; above operation
    mov     bl,6[di]            ;Load BL with the value
                                ; pointed to by DI + 6
    mov     cl,8 + [si] + table ;Load CL the value pointed
                                ; to by SI + table + 8
        .
        .
```

Based indexed addressing mode

Like the other indirect memory addressing modes, the based indexed addressing mode provides a pointer to a value and not the actual value itself. The following example illustrates the syntax for using the based indexed addressing mode:

```
[register][register]
or
[register + register]
```

Where:

register   is either register **BX, BP, DI,** or **SI.**

Note:

You must use one base register and one index register to reference data with the based indexed addressing mode.

The following example shows some assembly language statements that use the based indexed addressing mode:

```
        .
        .
mov     ax,[bx][si]              ;Load AX with the value
                                 ; pointed to by BX and SI
mov     [bp][di],al              ;Save AL as the value
                                 ; pointed to by BP and DI
add     dx,[bx + di]             ;Add the value pointed to
                                 ; by BX and DI to DX
        .
        .
```

The Based Indexed with Displacement Addressing Mode

Like the other three indirect memory addressing modes, the based indexed with displacement addressing mode provides a pointer to a value and not the actual value itself. The following example illustrates the syntax for using the based indexed with displacement addressing mode:

```
displacement[register][register]
or
[register + register + displacement]
```

Where:

displacement   is either a constant, a memory address, or both.

register   is either register **BX, BP, DI,** or **SI.**

Note:
As with the based indexed addressing mode, you must use one base register and one index register to reference data with the based indexed with displacement addressing mode.

The following example shows some assembly language statements that use the based indexed with displacement addressing mode:

```
        .
        .
        .
table       dp      1000 dup (?)
        .
        .
    mov     al,table[bx][si]        ;Load AL with the value
                                    ; pointe to by table + BX
                                    ; + SI
    mov     al,[table + bx + si] ;Does the same as the
                                    ; above operation
    add     ax,10[bp][di]           ;Add the value pointed to
                                    ; by BP + DI + 10 to AX

        .
        .
```

Summary

This chapter explained the variety of addressing modes that the 8088 microprocessor offers. These addressing modes enable you to reference data as constants, as variables in registers and memory, and through the use of pointers. All of these addressing modes conform quite well with what high-level programming languages offer.

Chapter 7

Structured Programming

You can adapt many of the most important high-level language programming techniques to 8088 assembly language programming by using structured programming techniques. Structured programming techniques simplify program implementation and they make programs much easier to read and maintain. Accordingly, it is essential to completely understand how to write 8088 assembly language programs using structured programming techniques if you want to become an efficient assembly language programmer. This chapter teaches you how you can write assembly language programs using three fairly simple control structures:

- sequencing
- selection
- repetition.

Sequencing

Sequencing is how a computer program executes one statement after another. Look at how a few simple assignment statements are executed in a C program:

```
a = b + 4;

c = c + 10 - a;
```

Through sequencing, the statement **a = b + 4** would be executed and then the statement **c = c + 10 - a** would be executed. Now look at how the same two assignment statements can be written in 8088 assembly language:

```
        .
        .
a       dw      ?
b       dw      ?
c       dw      ?
        .
        .
        mov     ax,b     ;AX = b
        add     ax,4     ;AX = b + 4
        mov     a,ax     ;a = b + 4
        mov     ax,c     ;AX = c
        add     ax,10    ;AX = c + 10
        sub     ax,a     ;AX = c + 10 - a
        mov     c,ax     ;c = c + 10 - a
        .
        .
```

Although the assembly language version of the assignment statements is longer, both versions of the assignment statements perform the same function and in the same order. As you can see from these two examples, sequencing provides an orderly flow from statement to statement. Without sequencing, programs would be chaotic.

Selection

Selection control structures allow program execution to branch away from the orderly flow of statements that sequencing provides. In high-level languages, such statements as **goto**, **if...then**, and **if...then...else** implement selection control structures. You can use the 8088 **JMP** instruction just like you use the **goto** instruction in a high-level language. Furthermore, you can use conditional jumps to simulate both the **if...then** and the **if...then...else** control structures the 8088 assembly language. First, look at a C **if...then** structure:

```
if ( a! =  b )

    c  =  3;
```

This simple **if...then** structure assigns a value of **3** to **c** if **a** does not equal **b**. Now look at an 8088 assembly language equivalent:

```
          .
          .
a         dw     ?
b         dw     ?
c         dw     ?
          .
          .
          mov    ax,a      ;AX = a
          cmp    ax,b      ;Is a equal to b?
          je     next      ;Jump if it is
          mov    c,3       ;c = 3
next:     .
          .
          .
```

Note how a **JE** instruction is used instead of a **JNE** instruction. In a case like the previous example, it is usually easier to use a conditional jump that is the opposite of the condition being tested for. Look at how a **JNE** instruction would have been used in the program:

```
            •
            •
a           dw      ?
b           dw      ?
c           dw      ?
            •
            •
            mov     ax,a        ;AX = a
            cmp     ax,b        ;Is a equal to b?
            jne     nequal      ;Jump if it isn't
            jmp     next        ;Jump over the next statement
nequal:     mov     c,3         ;c = 3
next:       •
            •
            •
```

Implementing an **if...then...else** control structure in 8088 assembly language is almost as simple as implementing an **if...then** control structure. First look at a fairly simple C **if...then...else** control structure:

```
if   ( a ! = b )

       c   =   3;

else

       c   =   4;
```

Like the previous example, this **if...then...else** statement assigns a value of **3** to **c** if **a** does not equal **b**. Otherwise, the **if...then...else** statement assigns a value of **4** to **c** if **a** is equal to **b**. Look at how the previous **if...then...else** statement could be written in 8088 assembly language:

```
           •
           •
a       dw      ?
b       dw      ?
c       dw      ?
           •
           •
        mov     ax,a            ;AX = a
        cmp     ax,b            ;Is a equal to b?
        jne     nequal          ;Jump if it isn't
        mov     c,4             ;c = 4
        jmp     next            ;Jump
nequal: mov     c,3             ;c = 3
next:      •
           •
           •
```

Repetition

A repetition control structure executes a statement or statements either endlessly or until a condition has been met. In high-level languages, repetition control structures are implemented with **for**, **while**, **repeat**, and **do** loops. As with sequencing and selection, it is fairly easy to implement repetition in an 8088 assembly language program.

The For Loop

Examine a simple **for** loop in a C program:

```
for  ( i = 0; i< 10; i++ )

    a++;
```

This **for** loop will loop 10 times and for each repetition **a** will be incremented. Look at how the same loop could be implemented in an assembly language program:

```
          .
          .
a     dw      ?
          .
          .
      mov     al,0     ;Initialize the counter
l1:   cmp     al,10    ;Jump if the
      jae     l2       ; loop is complete
      inc     a        ;Bump a
      inc     al       ;Bump the loop counter
      jmp     l1       ;Loop
l2:       .
          .
          .
```

Although the previous assembly language example gets the job done, it is mostly a literal translation of the C example before it. For that matter, the assembly language code is what you might expect to get out of a good optimizing C compiler. However, assembly language programming is one of the few remaining areas of computer programming that we can still do better than the machine can. Look at how the previous assembly language example could be improved:

```
        .
        .
a       dw      ?
        .
        .
        mov     cx,10    ;Initialize  the  loop  counter
l1:     inc     a        ;Bump a
        loop    l1       ;Loop till done
        .
        .
```

Notice how this loop requires only three instructions instead of the six that the previous example required. This version of the loop is vastly superior to its predecessor. Not only is the overall size of the program reduced, the fewer instructions inside of the loop significantly reduces execution time. Of course, you could go even further and accomplish the same result with one statement: add ax,10. However, the objective here is to illustrate how loops are constructed in 8088 assembly language rather than how compiler-generated code can be reduced to almost nothing.

The While Loop

Before you implement a **while** loop in assembly language, look at this **while** loop in C programming:

```
while   ( a ! = 10 )

        a++;
```

As you can see, this **while** loop continuously increments **a** until it is equal to **10**. Now look at how you can code the same **while** loop in 8088 assembly language:

```
        .
        .
a       dw      ?
        .
        .
l1:     cmp     a,10    ;Jump
        je      l2      ; if done
        inc     a       ;Bump a
        jmp     l1      ;Loop till done
l2:     .
        .
        .
```

The Do Loop

As a final look at how repetitive structures are coded in assembly language, look at a **do** loop in C programming:

```
    do

            a++;

    while ( a ! = 10 );
```

Like the **while** loop, this **do** loop increments **a** until it is equal to **10**. Look at how you could code the same loop in assembly language:

```
        .
        .
a       dw      ?
        .
        .
l1:     inc     a       ;Bump a
        cmp     a,10    ;Loop
        jne     l1      ; until done
        .
        .
```

Summary

In this chapter, you learned how you can use sequencing, selection, and repetition control structures in assembly language programming. The chapter also presented both high-level language examples and corresponding assembly language equivalents to further reinforce an understanding of these very important programming techniques.

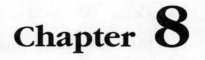

Chapter 8

Strings

I n most computer programs, the most important pieces of data are strings. This is true for programs written with a high-level language and for assembly language programs. Accordingly, the 8088 has a special set of instructions that are designed just for manipulating strings. This chapter teaches you how you can use these 8088 string instructions to

- move strings
- load strings
- store strings
- compare strings
- scan strings.

MOVS, MOVSB, and MOVSW Instructions

The **MOVS** (**move** string), **MOVSB** (**move** byte string), and **MOVSW** (**move** word string) instructions move strings from one location in memory to another. The source string for the move is pointed to by **DS:SI** and the destination address to move the string to is pointed to by **ES:DI**. After each movement instruction is executed, **DI** and **SI** are either incremented or decremented according to the value of the **direction** flag. If the **direction** flag has been cleared by the **CLD** instruction, registers **DI** and **SI** are incremented once for byte string moves or incremented twice for word string moves. Conversely, **DI** and **SI** are decremented twice for byte string moves or decremented twice for word string moves when the **direction** flag has been set by the **STD** instruction. The following example defines the syntax for the **MOVS** instruction:

```
movs      destination,source
```

Where:

destination   is the address to move the string to.

source   is the current location of the string. Note that a segment override operator can be used to override the default segment address.

Note:

In addition to indicating the addresses of the source string and the destination string, the operands also indicate whether the operation is to be a byte move or a word move.

The following example defines the syntax for the **MOVSB** instruction:

```
movsb
```

The following example defines the syntax for the **MOVSW** instruction:

```
movsw
```

170

The following example shows some assembly language statements that use the **MOVS** instruction:

```
            •
            •
_DATA    segment   word public 'DATA'
srcstr   db        10 dup (?)
desstr   db        10 dup (?)
_DATA    ends
            •
            •
_TEXT    segment   word public 'CODE'
         assume    cs:_TEXT,ds:_DATA,es:_DATA
            •
            •
         mov       ax,_DATA      ;Set
         mov       ds,ax         ; both
         mov       es,ax         ; DS and ES
         lea       si,srcstr     ;DS:SI = Source string
                                 ; pointer
         lea       di,desstr     ;ES:DI = Destination
                                 ; pointer
         mov       cx,10         ;CX = Loop counter
         cld                     ;Clear the direction flag
l1:      movs      desstr,srcstr ;Move a byte of data
         loop      l1            ;Loop till the string is
                                 ; moved
            •
            •
```

The previous program fragment simply moves a string of 10 characters from one memory location to another.

The following program fragment accomplishes the same task, but uses the **MOVSB** instruction instead of the **MOVS** instruction:

```
                •
                •
_DATA    segment   word public 'DATA'
srcstr   db        10 dup (?)
desstr   db        10 dup (?)
_DATA    ends
                •
                •
_TEXT    segment   word public 'CODE'
         assume    cs:_TEXT,ds:_DATA,es:_DATA
                •
                •
         mov       ax,_DATA        ;Set
         mov       ds,ax           ; both
         mov       es,ax           ; DS and ES
         lea       si,srcstr       ;DS:SI = Source string
                                   ; pointer
         lea       di,desstr       ;ES:DI = Destination
                                   ; pointer
         mov       cx,10           ;CX = Loop counter
         cld                       ;Clear the direction flag
l1:      movsb                     ;Move a byte of data
         loop      l1              ;Loop till the string is
                                   ; moved
                •
                •
```

As you can see, the previous program fragment is not much different from the example before it. The following program fragment is similar to the first two examples except that it moves a string of five words from one memory location to another:

```
            •
            •
_DATA    segment   word public 'DATA'
srcstr   dw        5 dup (?)
desstr   dw        5 dup (?)
_DATA    ends
            •
            •
_TEXT    segment   word public 'CODE'
         assume    cs:_TEXT,ds:_DATA,es:_DATA
            •
            •
         mov       ax,_DATA         ;Set
         mov       ds,ax            ; both
         mov       es,ax            ; DS and ES
         lea       si,srcstr        ;DS:SI = Source string
                                    ; pointer
         lea       di,desstr        ;ES:DI = Destination
                                    ; pointer
         mov       cx,5             ;CX = Loop counter
         cld                        ;Clear the direction flag
l1:      movsw                      ;Move a byte of data
         loop      l1               ;Loop till the string is
                                    ; moved
            •
            •
```

The REP Prefix

The 8088 provides the **REP** (**rep**eat) prefix to simplify using the string instructions. Whenever an 8088 string instruction is preceded with a **REP** prefix, the **CX** register is decremented after each instruction. If **CX** is not equal to 0, the string instruction is executed again. Otherwise, the repetition of the string instruction ceases if **CX** reaches 0. Essentially, the **REP** prefix simply eliminates the need for a **LOOP** instruction. The following program fragment is the same as the previous **MOVSW** example except that this version uses the **REP** prefix instead of a **LOOP** instruction:

```
            .
            .
_DATA     segment   word public 'DATA'
srcstr    dw        5 dup (?)
desstr    dw        5 dup (?)
_DATA     ends
            .
            .
_TEXT     segment   word public 'CODE'
          assume    cs:_TEXT,ds:_DATA,es:_DATA
            .
            .
          mov       ax,_DATA        ;Set
          mov       ds,ax           ;both
          mov       es,ax           ;DS and ES
          lea       si,srcstr       ;DS:SI = Source string
                                    ; pointer
          lea       di,desstr       ;ES:DI = Destination
                                    ; pointer
          mov       cx,5            ;CX = Loop counter
          cld                       ;Clear the direction flag
          rep       movsw           ;Move the string
            .
            .
```

LODS, LODSB, and LODSW Instructions

The **LODS** (**load** string), **LODSB** (**load b**yte string), and **LODSW** (**load w**ord string) instructions load either a byte or word value into the accumulator (register **AL** or **AX**). The string is pointed to by **DS:SI**. After each load instruction is executed, **SI** is either incremented or decremented according to the value of the **direction** flag. If the **direction** flag has been cleared by the **CLD** instruction, register **SI** is incremented once for byte string loads or incremented twice for word string moves. Conversely, **SI** is decremented once for byte string moves or decremented twice for word string moves when the direction flag has been set by the **STD** instruction. The following example defines the syntax for the **LODS** instruction:

lods   source

Where:

source   is the current location of the string.
                        You can use a segment override operator
                        to override the default segment ad-
                        dress.

Note:

In addition to indicating the string's current address, the
source operand also indicates whether a byte or a word is
to be moved into the appropriate accumulator.

The following example defines the syntax for the **LODSB** instruction:

lodsb

The following example defines the syntax for the **LODSW** instruction:

lodsw

The following example shows some assembly language statements that use the **LODS** instruction:

```
                .
                .
_DATA    segment   word public 'DATA'
scores   db        10 dup (?)
_DATA    ends
                .
                .
_TEXT    segment   word public 'CODE'
         assume    cs:_TEXT,ds:_DATA
                .
                .
         mov       ax,_DATA        ;Set
         mov       ds,ax           ; DS
         lea       si,scores       ;DS:SI = Source pointer
         mov       cx,10           ;CX = Loop counter
         mov       bl,0            ;BL = Total
         cld                       ;Flag increment
l1:      lods      scores          ;AL = Next byte
         add       bl,al           ;Adjust the total
         loop      l1              ;Loop till done
                .
                .
```

The previous program fragment uses the **LODS** instruction to figure the total for 10-byte values. The following program fragment accomplishes the same task as the previous program, but uses the **LODSB** instruction instead of the **LODS** instruction:

```
           .
           .
_DATA    segment   word public 'DATA'
scores   db        10 dup (?)
_DATA    ends
           .

           .
_TEXT    segment   word public 'CODE'
         assume    cs:_TEXT,ds:_DATA
           .

           .
         mov       ax,_DATA        ;Set
         mov       ds,ax           ; DS
         lea       si,scores       ;DS:SI = Source pointer
         mov       cx,10           ;CX = Loop counter
         mov       bl,0            ;BL = Total
         cld                       ;Flag increment
l1:      lodsb                     ;AL = Next byte
         add       bl,al           ;Adjust the total
         loop      l1              ;Loop till done
           .

           .
```

177

The following program fragment is similar to the previous two examples except that it calculates the total for five words of data:

```
                .
                .
        _DATA   segment  word public 'DATA'
        scores  dw       5 dup (?)
        _DATA   ends
                .
                .
        _TEXT   segment  word public 'CODE'
                assume   cs:_TEXT,ds:_DATA
                .
                .
                mov      ax,_DATA       ;Set
                mov      ds,ax          ;DS
                lea      si,scores      ;DS:SI = Source pointer
                mov      cx,5           ;CX = Loop counter
                mov      bx,0           ;BX = Total
                cld                     ;Flag increment
        l1:     lodsw                   ;AX = Next byte
                add      bx,ax          ;Adjust the total
                loop     l1             ;Loop till done
                .
                .
```

STOS, STOSB, and STOSW Instructions

The **STOS** (store string), **STOSB** (store byte string), and **STOSW** (store word string) instructions store either a byte or word value into a string location. The string is pointed to by **ES:DI** and the value to be stored is expected to be in the appropriate accumulator (register **AL** or **AX**). After each store instruction is executed, **DI** is either incremented or decremented according to the value of the **direction** flag. If the **direction** flag is cleared by the **CLD** instruction, register **DI** is incremented once for byte string stores or incremented twice for word string stores. Conversely, **DI** is decremented once for byte string stores or decremented twice for word string stores when the direction flag has been set by the **STD** instruction. The following example defines the syntax for the **STOS** instruction:

```
stos          destination
Where:
destination        is the current location of the string.

Note:
In addition to indicating the current address of the
string, the destination operand also indicates whether a
byte or a word is to be moved from the appropriate accumu-
lator.
```

The following example defines the syntax for the **STOSB** instruction:

```
stosb
```

The following example defines the syntax for the **STOSW** instruction:

```
stosw
```

8 Strings

The following example shows some assembly language statements that use the **STOS** instruction:

```
              •
              •
_DATA   segment   word public 'DATA'
buffer  db        10 dup (?)
_DATA   ends
              •
              •
_TEXT   segment   word public 'CODE'
        assume    cs:_TEXT,ds:_DATA
              •
              •
        mov       ax,_DATA      ;Set
        mov       es,ax         ;ES
        lea       di,buffer     ;ES:DI = Buffer pointer
        mov       cx,10         ;CX = Loop counter
        mov       al,0          ;AL = Value to be stored
        cld                     ;Flag increment
ll:     stos      buffer        ;Save a 0
        loop      ll            ;Loop till done
              •
              •
```

The previous program fragment uses the **STOS** instruction to zero out a 10-byte long buffer. The following program fragment accomplishes the same task as the previous example but uses the **STOSB** instruction instead of the **STOS** instruction:

```
        .
        .
_DATA   segment  word public 'DATA'
buffer  dw       5 dup (?)
_DATA   ends
        .
        .
_TEXT   segment  word public 'CODE'
        assume   cs:_TEXT,ds:_DATA
        .
        .
        mov      ax,_DATA        ;Set
        mov      es,ax           ;ES
        lea      di,buffer       ;ES:DI = Buffer pointer
        mov      cx,5            ;CX = Loop counter
        mov      ax,0            ;AX = Value to be stored
        cld                      ;Flag increment
l1:     stosw                    ;Save a 0
        loop     l1              ;Loop till done
        .
        .
```

The following program fragment is similar to the previous two examples except that it zeros out a buffer of five words:

```
        .
        .
_DATA   segment  word public 'DATA'
buffer  db       10 dup (?)
_DATA   ends
        .
        .
_TEXT   segment  word public 'CODE'
        assume   cs:_TEXT,ds:_DATA
        .
        .
        mov      ax,_DATA        ;Set
        mov      es,ax           ;ES
        lea      di,buffer       ;ES:DI = Buffer pointer
        mov      cx,10           ;CX = Loop counter
        mov      al,0            ;AL = Value to be stored
        cld                      ;Flag increment
l1:     stosb                    ;Save a 0
        loop     l1              ;Loop till done
        .
        .
```

The REP Prefix

As with the **MOVS** family of instructions, you can use the **REP** prefix to simplify using the **STOS** family of instructions. The following program fragment is similar to the **STOSW** example except that this version uses the **REP** prefix instead of a **LOOP** instruction:

```
        .
        .
_DATA   segment   word public 'DATA'
buffer  dw        5 dup (?)
_DATA   ends
        .
        .
_TEXT   segment   word public 'CODE'
        assume    cs:_TEXT,ds:_DATA
        .
        .
        mov       ax,_DATA        ;Set
        mov       es,ax           ;ES
        lea       di,buffer       ;ES:DI = Buffer pointer
        mov       cx,5            ;CX = Loop counter
        mov       ax,0            ;AX = Value to be stored
        cld                       ;Flag increment
        rep       stosw           ;Zero out the buffer
        .
        .
```

CMPS, CMPSB, and CMPSW Instructions

The **CMPS** (**comp**are string), **CMPSB** (**comp**are **b**yte string), and **CMPSW** (**comp**are word string) instructions compare strings. The source string for the comparison is pointed to by **DS:SI** and the destination string is pointed to by **ES:DI**. The strings are compared either a byte or word at a time with the destination value being compared to the source value. After each comparison, the flags are updated appropriately and registers **DI** and **SI** are either incremented or decremented according to the value of the **direction** flag. If the **direction** flag has been cleared by the **CLD** instruction, registers **DI** and **SI** are incremented once for byte string comparisons or incremented twice for word string comparisons. Conversely, **DI** and **SI** are decremented once for byte string comparisons or decremented twice for word string comparisons when the **direction** flag has been set by the **STD** instruction. The following example defines the syntax for the **CMPS** instruction:

```
cmps          source,destination
Where:
destination        is the address of the string to be
                   compared with the source string.
source             is the address of the source string.
                   Note that a segment override operator
                   can be used to override the default
                   segment address.
```

Note:

```
In addition to indicating the addresses of the source
string and the destination string, the operands also indi-
cate whether the operation will be a byte comparison or a
word comparison.
```

The following example defines the syntax for the **CMPSB** instruction:

```
cmpsb
```

The following example defines the syntax for the **CMPSW** instruction:

```
cmpsw
```

The following example shows some assembly language statements that use the **CMPS** instruction:

```
        .
        .
_DATA   segment   word public 'DATA'
srcstr  db        10 dup (?)
desstr  db        10 dup (?)
_DATA   ends
        .
        .
_TEXT   segment   word public 'CODE'
        assume    cs:_TEXT,ds:_DATA,es:_DATA
        .
        .
        mov       ax,_DATA        ;Set
        mov       ds,ax           ;both
        mov       es,ax           ;DS and ES
        lea       si,srcstr       ;DS:SI = Source string
                                  ; pointer
        lea       di,desstr       ;ES:DI = Destination
                                  ; string pointer
        mov       cx,10           ;CX = String length
        cld                       ;Flag increment
l1:     cmps      srcstr,desstr   ;Compare the strings
        jne       next            ;Jump if the bytes aren't
                                  ; the same
        loop      l1              ;Loop till the end of the
                                  ; strings
next:   .
        .
        .
```

The previous program fragment simply compares two 10-byte strings. The following program fragment accomplishes the same task, but uses the **CMPSB** instruction instead of the **CMPS** instruction:

```
                .
                .

_DATA    segment   word public 'DATA'
srcstr   db        10 dup (?)
desstr   db        10 dup (?)
_DATA    ends
                .
                .

_TEXT    segment   word public 'CODE'
         assume    cs:_TEXT,ds:_DATA,es:_DATA
                .
                .
         mov       ax,_DATA        ;Set
         mov       ds,ax           ;both
         mov       es,ax           ;DS and ES
         lea       si,srcstr       ;DS:SI = Source string
                                   ; pointer
         lea       di,desstr       ;ES:DI = Destination
                                   ;string pointer
         mov       cx,10           ; CX = String length
         cld                       ;Flag increment
l1:      cmpsb                     ;Compare the strings
         jne       next            ;Jump if the bytes aren't
                                   ; the same
         loop      l1              ;Loop till the end of the
                                   ; strings
next:           .
                .
                .
```

The following program fragment is similar to the previous two examples except that it compares strings of five words each:

```
           •
           •
_DATA      segment   word public 'DATA'
srcstr     dw        5 dup (?)
desstr     dw        5 dup (?)
_DATA      ends
           •
           •
_TEXT      segment   word public 'CODE'
           assume    cs:_TEXT,ds:_DATA,es:_DATA
           •
           •
           mov       ax,_DATA        ;Set
           mov       ds,ax           ; both
           mov       es,ax           ; DS and ES
           lea       si,srcstr       ;DS:SI = Source string
                                     ; pointer
           lea       di,desstr       ;ES:DI = Destination string
                                     ; pointer
           mov       cx,5            ;CX = String length
           cld                       ;Flag increment
ll:        cmpsw                     ;Compare the strings
           jne       next            ;Jump if the words aren't
                                     ; the same
           loop      ll              ;Loop till the end of the
                                     ; strings
next:      •
           •
           •
```

The REPE and REPNE Prefixes

In addition to the **REP** prefix, the 8088 provides the **REPE** (or **REPZ**) and the **REPNE** (or **REPNZ**) prefixes to simplify using the **CMPS** family of instructions. Whenever an 8088 string instruction is preceded by the **REPE** prefix, the **CX** register is decremented and the **zero** flag is checked. If **CX** is equal to 0 or the **zero** flag has been set by the comparison, the repetition of the string instruction is halted. Otherwise, the repetition of the string instruction continues while **CX** is not equal to 0 or the **zero** flag is not set. If a string instruction is preceded by the **REPNE** prefix, the **CX** register is decremented and the **zero** flag is checked. If **CX** is equal to 0 or the **zero** flag has not been set by the comparison, the repetition of the string instruction is halted. Otherwise, the repetition of the string instruction continues while **CX** is not equal to 0 or the **zero** flag is set. The following program fragment is the same as the previous **CMPSW** example except that this version uses the **REPE** instruction instead of the **LOOP** instruction:

```
        .
        .

_DATA   segment   word public 'DATA'
srcstr  dw        5 dup (?)
desstr  dw        5 dup (?)
_DATA   ends
        .
        .

_TEXT   segment   word public 'CODE'
        assume    cs:_TEXT,ds:_DATA,es:_DATA
        .
        .

        mov       ax,_DATA       ;Set
        mov       ds,ax          ; both
        mov       es,ax          ; DS and ES
        lea       si,srcstr      ;DS:SI = Source string
                                 ; pointer
        lea       di,desstr      ;ES:DI = Destination string
                                 ; pointer
```

continued...

...from previous page

```
mov    cx,5                 ;CX = String length
cld                         ;Flag increment
repe   cmpw                 ;Compare the strings
  .
  .
```

SCAS, SCASB, and SCASW Instructions

The **SCAS** (**scan** string), **SCASB** (**scan** byte string), and **SCASW** (**scan** word string) instructions scan a string for a value specified in the accumulator (register **AL** or **AX**). The string is pointed to by **ES:DI**. The string is scanned either a byte at a time or a word at a time with the string value being compared to the accumulator. After each comparison, the flags are updated appropriately and register **DI** is either incremented or decremented according to the value of the **direction** flag. If the **direction** flag was cleared by the **CLD** instruction, register **DI** is incremented once for byte string scans or incremented twice for word string scans. Conversely, **DI** is decremented once for byte string scans or decremented twice for word string scans when the **direction** flag has been set by **STD** instruction. The following example defines the syntax for the **SCAS** instruction:

```
scas          destination
```
Where:

```
destination          is the address of the string to be
                     scanned with the value in the accumula-
                     tor.
```

Note:

```
In addition to indicating the address of the destination
string, the operand also indicates whether the operation is
to be a byte scan or a word scan.
```

The following example defines the syntax for the **SCASB** instruction:

```
scasb
```

The following example defines the syntax for the **SCASW** instruction:

```
scasw
```

The following program fragment is an example of how an assembly language program uses the **SCAS** instruction:

```
        .
        .
_DATA   segment  word public 'DATA'
string  db       10 dup (?)
_DATA   ends
        .

        .
_TEXT   segment  word public 'CODE'
        assume   cs:_TEXT,ds:_DATA,es:_DATA
        .

        .
        mov      ax,_DATA          ;Set
        mov      es,ax             ;ES
        lea      di,string         ;ES:DI = String pointer
        mov      cx,10             ;CX = String length
        cld                        ;Flag increment
        mov      al,0ffh           ;AL = Value to scan for
ll:     scas     string            ;Compare the string byte
                                   ; with AL
        je       next              ;Jump if 0FFh is found
        loop     ll                ;Continue with the scan
next:   .
        .
        .
```

As you can see, the previous program fragment simply scans a 10-byte string for the value 0FFH. The following program fragment accomplishes the same task, but uses the **SCASB** instruction instead of the **SCAS** instruction:

```
        .
        .
_DATA   segment   word public 'DATA'
string  db        10 dup (?)
_DATA   ends
        .
        .
_TEXT   segment   word public 'CODE'
        assume    cs:_TEXT,ds:_DATA,es:_DATA
        .
        .
        mov       ax,_DATA        ;Set
        mov       es,ax           ;ES
        lea       di,string       ;ES:DI = String pointer
        mov       cx,10           ;CX = String length
        cld                       ;Flag increment
        mov       al,0ffh         ;AL = Value to scan for
l1:     scasb                     ;Compare the string word
                                  ;with AX
        je        next            ;Jump if 0FFh is found
        loop      l1              ;Continue with the scan
next:   .
        .
        .
```

8 Strings

The following program fragment is similar to the two previous examples except that it uses the **SCASW** instruction to scan a string of five words:

```
                .
                .
    _DATA   segment   word public 'DATA'
    string  dw        5 dup (?)
    _DATA   ends
                .
                .
    _TEXT   segment   word public 'CODE'
            assume    cs:_TEXT,ds:_DATA,es:_DATA
                .
                .
            mov       ax,_DATA          ;Set
            mov       es,ax             ; ES
            lea       di,string         ;ES:DI = String pointer
            mov       cx,5              ;CX = String length
            cld                         ;Flag increment
            mov       AX,03effh         ;AX = Value to scan for
    l1:     scasw                       ;Compare the string byte
                                        ; with AL
            je        next              ;Jump if 03eFFh is found
            loop      l1                ;Continue with the scan
    next:       .
                .
                .
```

The REPE and REPNE Prefixes

Like the CMPS family of instructions, the **REPE** and the **REPNE** instructions simplify using the **SCAS** family of instructions. The following program fragment is similar to the **SCASW** example except that this version uses the **REPNE** prefix instead of a **LOOP** instruction:

```
        .
        .
_DATA   segment   word public 'DATA'
string  dw        5 dup (?)
_DATA   ends
        .
        .
_TEXT   segment   word public 'CODE'
        assume    cs:_TEXT,ds:_DATA,es:_DATA
        .
        .
        mov       ax,_DATA        ;Set
        mov       es,ax           ; ES
        lea       di,string       ;ES:DI = String pointer
        mov       cx,5            ;CX = String length
        cld                       ;Flag increment
        mov       AX,03effh       ;AX = Value to scan for
        repne     scasw           ;Compare the string word
                                  ; with AX
        .
        .
```

Summary

This chapter explained the string instructions that are available to you. These instructions perform operations, such as, moving strings, loading strings, storing strings, comparing strings, and scanning strings. Additionally, this chapter showed you how you can use the 8088 repeat prefixes in conjunction with the string instructions to simplify program implementation.

Chapter 9

Structures and Records

A lthough numeric and string data types are the most common types of data a program processes, many types of data can only be represented by using a combination of other data types. This chapter teaches you about

- structures, which represent a diverse range of data types
- records, which make it easier for you to write programs that manipulate bits.

Structures

The 8088 assembly language provides structures to make a totally new data type from a combination of other data types. The first step in using an assembly language structure is to define the structure type. You define a structure type by creating a template for the structure. The following example defines the syntax for creating a structure type template:

```
name  stru
field declaration
     .

     .

field declaration
name  ends
Where:
name              is the name of the structure type.
field declaration  is a field declaration.
```

As the previous example illustrates, a structure type definition is constructed from a number of field declarations. These field declarations use the same syntax as data declarations use. Look at what a structure type definition looks like for a structure that holds a person's first name, last name, month of birth, day of birth, and year of birth:

```
person  struc
fname   db    'First name goes here'
lname   db    'Last name goes here'
month   dw    ?
day     dw    ?
year    dw    ?
person  ends
```

Note that each field declaration has a name. A field name can be any legitimate identifier name except that it must not be used anywhere else in the assembly language program. Consequently, a program that uses the previous structure cannot use **fname** as a variable identifier elsewhere in the program. Also, note that a field can be assigned a default value and string fields should be long enough to hold the longest string that the field is expected to hold.

Structure Variables

When you define a structure type, you can use it in a program by defining a structure variable. The following example presents the syntax for defining a structure variable:

```
name       strucname  initial value, initial value
```

Where:

```
name                is the identifier of the variable.
strucname           is the name of the structure type.
initial value       is the initial value of the field.
```

As the previous example illustrates, you can specify initial values for a structure variable's fields in the structure variable declaration. A field's default value is used if you do not specify an initial value in the structure variable declaration. The following example shows some structure variable declarations:

```
p1       person           <'John', 'Smith', 2, 4, 81>
p2       person           <'Jane', 'Doe', , 12, 83>
```

Note how the second example does not supply an initial **month** value. Therefore, **p2**'s **month** field is undefined because the **month** field's default value is **?**. Also, note that a field with more than one default value cannot be overridden with an initial value in the structure variable declaration. Examine the following structure type definition:

```
person     struc
fname      db     'First name goes here'
lname      db     'Last name goes here'
birthday   dw     3 dup (?)
person     ends
```

As you can see, this new structure type is a slight revision of the previous **person** structure type. However, this new structure type combines the three birth date values into a single field. Although you can still initialize the first two fields in the structure variable declaration, you cannot initialize the **birthday** field because it has multiple values. Consequently, the **birthday** field will always be assigned the default value for any variables that are declared with the new **person** structure type.

Referencing Structure Fields

Now that you can define a structure type and declare variables with the created structure's type, examine how the value of a field is referenced in an assembly language instruction. The following example illustrates how a structure's field is referenced:

```
variable.field
```
Where:

```
variable        is the name of the variable.
field           is the name of the field.
```

To better illustrate how structures are used in an assembly language program, the following program fragment performs a variety of operations on a structure that is declared with the original **person** structure type:

```
            .
            .
person      struc
fname       db          'First name goes here'
lname       db          'Last name goes here '
month       dw          ?
day         dw          ?
year        dw          ?
person      ends
            .
            .
_DATA       segment     word public 'DATA'
somebody    person      <'John', , , , >
continued...
```

...from previous page

```
last      db          'Doe'
_DATA     ends
          .
          .

_TEXT     segment     word public 'CODE'
          assume      cs:_TEXT,ds:_DATA,es:_DATA
          mov         ax,_DATA                ;Set
          mov         ds,ax                   ; both
          mov         es,ax                   ; DS and ES
          mov         si,offset last          ;DS:SI = The person's
                                              ; last name string
          mov         di,offset somebody.lname ;ES:DI = Destina
                                              ; tion pointer
          mov         cx,3                    ;CX = String length
          cld                                 ;Flag increment
          rep         movsb                   ;Save the new last
                                              ; name
          mov         somebody.month,10       ;Set the person's
                                              ; birth month
          mov         dx,9                    ;Set the
          mov         somebody.day,dx         ;Set the person's
                                              ; birthday
          mov         somebody.year,1990      ;Set the person's
                                              ; birth year
          .
          .
```

Records

As structures require a type definition before you can use them in an assembly language program, records also require a type definition before you can use them. To define a record type, you create a template. A template for a record type is similar to a structure template except that a record deals with bits and not a variety of data types. The following example defines the syntax for creating a record type template:

```
name        record      field, field
```
Where:
```
name                is the name of the record type.
field               is a field declaration.
```

As the previous example illustrates, a record type definition requires one or more field declarations. These field declarations specify the width of a field and an optional default value. When creating a record type, you must keep in mind that the maximum number of bits in a record type is 16. If a record type uses eight or fewer bits, its variables are stored as a byte value. If a record type uses more than eight bits, its variables are stored as a word. The following example defines the syntax for declaring a field's width and optional default value:

```
name:width=expression
```
Where:
```
name                is the name of the field.
width               is the width of the field.
expression          is an optional default value for the
                    field.
```

To better illustrate how you can put a record type to practical use in an assembly language program, look at how the IBM PC color codes are stored in a byte value. The following example illustrates how the information is stored in an IBM PC color code byte:

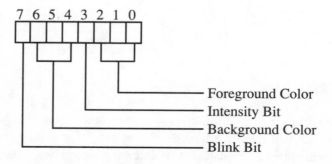

As the previous example illustrates, an IBM PC color code byte is an ideal candidate for a record type. You could use the following definition to define a record type for a color code byte:

```
colorcode       record      blink:1,back:3,intensity:1,fore:3
```

Record Variables

When you define a record type, you can use it in an assembly language program to define a record variable. The following example presents the syntax for defining a record variable:

```
name      recordname <initial value,  initial value,etc.>
Where:
name                 is the identifier of the variable.
recordname           is the name of the record type.
initial value        is a initial value of the field.
```

As the previous example illustrates, you can specify initial values for a record variable's fields in the record variable declaration. If you do not specify an initial value in the record variable declaration, the field's default value is used. The following example shows some record variable declarations:

```
c1        color      <0,0,1,5>
array     color      20 dup (<>)
c2        color      <1,2,1,7>
```

To better illustrate how records are used in an assembly language program, the following program fragment performs a variety operations with operands and variables of the record type **colorcode**:

```
            .
            .
colorcode   record      blink:1,back:3,intensity:1,fore:3
            .
            .
_DATA       segment     word public 'DATA'
c1          colorcode   <0,3,1,6>
_DATA       ends
            .
            .
_TEXT       segment     word public 'CODE'
            assume      cs:_TEXT,ds:_DATA
            mov         ax,_DATA                ;Set
            mov         ds,ax                   ; DS
            mov         al,c1                   ;Load AL with the
                                                ; color code
            mov         ah,color <1,3,1,5> ;Load AH with a
                                                ; color code
            mov         c1,ah                   ;Save the new
                                                ; color code
            .
            .
```

Note that the expression **color <1,3,1,5>** is used as an operand in the previous program fragment. Not only can records be used as operands, the 8088 assembly language has two operators just for working with records in expressions: **MASK** and **WIDTH**.

The MASK Operator

The **MASK** operator returns a bit mask for a specified record field. The resulting mask returns a result with all of the field's bits set to 1. Any of the bits that are not in the field are returned with a value of 0. Additionally, the **MASK** operator can return a bit mask for an entire record. As with a field result, all bits contained in the record are returned with a 1 and any bits not in the record are returned with a 0. The following example defines the syntax for the MASK operator:

```
mask          field name or record
Where:
field name              is the name of the desired field.

record                  is a previously defined record vari-
                        able.
```

The following program fragment illustrates how you can use the **MASK** operator in an assembly language program:

```
              .
              .
colorcode record      blink:1,back:3,intensity:1,fore:3
              .

              .
_DATA     segment   word public 'DATA'
cl        colorcode <1,0,1,5>
_DATA     ends
              .

              .
_TEXT     segment   word public 'CODE'
          assume    cs:_TEXT,ds:_DATA
              .

              .
          mov       al,cl                     ;AL = Color
                                              ; code
          and       al,not mask blink         ;Turn off the
                                              ; blinking
          and       al,not mask intensity     ;Turn off the
                                              ; intensity
              .

              .
```

The WIDTH Operator

The **WIDTH** operator returns the number of bits in either a field or a record. The following example defines the syntax for the **WIDTH** operator:

```
width    field name or record
Where:
field name          is the name of the desired field.
record              is a previously defined record vari-
                    able.
```

The following program fragment illustrates how you can use the **WIDTH** operator in an assembly language program:

```
            .
            .
colorcode   record    blink:1,back:3,intensity:1,fore:3
            .
            .
_TEXT       segment   word public 'CODE'
            assume    cs:_TEXT,ds:_DATA
            .
            .
            mov       al,width blink     ;AL = Blink width
            add       al,width back      ;AL = Blink width +
                                         ; back width
            .
            .
```

Referencing Record Fields

Whenever you use a record field as an operand, it returns the location of the field's least significant bit. For example, the **colorcode**'s **fore** field would return a value of 0, its **intensity** field would return a value of 3, its **back** field would return a value of 4, and its **blink** field would return a value of 7. The following program fragment illustrates how you can use a record field's location in an assembly language program:

```
           .
           .
colorcode  record     blink:1,back:3,intensity:1,fore:3
           .
           .
_DATA      segment    word public 'DATA'
cl         colorcode  <1,0,1,5>
_DATA      ends
           .
           .
_TEXT      segment    word public 'CODE'
           assume     cs:_TEXT,ds:_DATA
           .
           .
           mov        al,cl           ;AL = Color code
           and        al,mask back    ;Strip away all but
                                       ; the background
           mov        cl,back         ;CL = Background
                                       ; position
           shr        al,cl           ;Move it to the
                                       ; byte's least sig-
                                       ; nificant bits
           .
           .
```

Summary

In this chapter, you learned about 8088 assembly language structures and records. You have seen how you can use structures to combine a variety of data types into a single data type and how you can use records to combine bit strings into both byte and word values. Additionally, this chapter taught you how you can use the **MASK** and **WIDTH** operators to manipulate records.

Chapter 10

Stacks

This chapter teaches you about one of the most important aspects of 8088 assembly language programming: the stack. You use stacks for one main purpose: to temporarily store data by both the 8088 microprocessor and the assembly language program. For now, focus on studying how an assembly language program uses a stack.

The Stack

All assembly language programs need to set aside an area of memory called the stack. This stack area is located in memory at the segment address pointed to by segment register **SS**. To better understand how this special area of memory is used, consider how a stack of paper is created. You simply stack one piece of paper on top of another. As a result, you form a stack of paper from the bottom upward. To retrieve a certain piece of paper from the stack, you remove papers from the top working downward until you locate the desired paper.

For the most part, a computer stack functions the same way that a paper stack does. The major difference between a computer stack and a paper one is the direction that the stack is built. Unlike how the paper stack builds upward, a computer stack builds downward. Although this may not seem logical, it's really the most efficient way for a computer to build a stack. The reason for the computer's backward way of building stacks is a result of the way a computer loads a program into memory.

When a computer loads a program into memory, the program's executable code usually comes first. The code section is followed by a chunk of memory set aside for data. Since most programs do not know just how much memory to allocate until runtime, it is unsafe to put anything else into memory right after the data section of the program. This allows the data section to grow according to the program's dynamic runtime needs. So where does the stack go? Simple, it's put in high memory. From there it can build downward. Of course, it is possible for the data section that's building upward to collide with the stack that's building downward. However, you should not expect this situation because as you gain experience in assembly language programming, you will learn to allocate a reasonable amount of memory for a program's stack segment. The following example illustrates the relationship between a program's code, data, and stack segments:

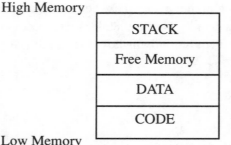

Figure 10-1. How a Computer Program Uses Memory.

Placing Data On and Off the Stack

As you have learned, the stack builds downward as data is placed on it. To maintain order in the stack, the **SP** register always points to the last data element that was placed on the stack. Note that only a 16-bit word can be placed on an 8088 stack. To place a word on the stack, the 8088 supplies the **PUSH** instruction. The following example defines the syntax for using the **PUSH** instruction:

```
push        operand
Where:
operand           is AX, BX, CX, DX, SP, BP, SI, DI, ES,
                  CS, SS, DS, or Mem16.
```

A 16-bit word can be removed from the bottom (or top, depending on your point of view) of the stack by using the 8088 **POP** instruction. The following example defines the syntax for the **POP** instruction:

```
pop         operand
Where:
operand           is AX, BX, CX, DX, SP, BP, SI, DI, ES,
                  CS, SS, DS, or Mem16.
```

The following program fragment shows how assembly language programs use the **PUSH** and **POP** instructions:

```
        .
        .
push    ax        ;Save AX
push    bx        ;Save BX

        .
        .
mov     ax,33     ;AX = 33
mov     bx,45     ;BX = 45
add     ax,bx     ;AX = 33 + 45

        .
        .
pop     bx        ;Restore BX
pop     ax        ;Restore AX

        .
        .
```

The previous program fragment simply saves registers **BX** and **AX** on the stack and, after performing a few operations with them, retrieves their former values from the stack. It's important to note from this example that values must be **POP**ped off the stack in the reverse order in which they were **PUSH**ed on to the stack. Remember that the **POP** instruction simply retrieves the data value that is on the bottom of the stack. Therefore, the last value put on the stack must be the first value retrieved from the stack.

The Flags and the Stack

In addition to being able to push and pop data values on and off the stack, the 8088 has two special instructions for pushing and popping the flags on and off the stack. These two instructions are the **PUSHF** and **POPF** instructions. The following example defines the syntax for the **PUSHF** instruction:

```
pushf
```

The following example defines the syntax for the **POPF** instruction:

```
popf
```

The following program fragment shows how assembly language programs use the **PUSHF** and **POPF** instructions:

```
        .
        .
pushf           ;Save the flags
add     ax,33   ;Add 33 to AX
popf            ;Restore the flags to the former values
        .
        .
```

Summary

In this chapter, you learned how the computer sets aside a special section of memory for a stack. Additionally, you learned how data and the flags can be temporarily saved on and retrieved off the stack.

Chapter 11

Procedures

Most modern high-level languages use procedures, functions, or both to modularize a program's code. Furthermore, procedures and functions can save a lot of space because a program can repeatedly call them at different points in its execution. This chapter teaches you

- how you can use assembly language procedures like high-level language procedures and functions to eliminate redundant code throughout the program

- how you can use the three methods for passing arguments to an assembly language procedure.

An Assembly Language Procedure

An assembly language procedure is a section of code that performs a specific purpose. You use the **PROC** and **ENDP** directives to create procedures in an assembly language program. The following example shows how you use the **PROC** and **ENDP** directives to define a procedure:

```
name      proc        type
          instruction
          .
          .
          instruction
name      endp
```

Where:

name	is the name of the procedure.
type	is either **NEAR** or **FAR**. If omitted, the procedure is assumed to be a **NEAR** procedure. You must specify **FAR** if the procedure will be called as a far call. Note that these assumptions do not apply if you are using an assembler that supports simplified segment directives and you are not using full segment definitions.
instruction	is an assembly language code statement.

Linkage

Simply defining a procedure is not enough. You must have a method for branching program execution to the procedure and returning from the procedure once it has completed its appointed task. Although you can use **JMP** statements to enter and exit from a procedure, it is very inefficient to use them for linking one part of the program with another. The preferred method for branching program execution to a procedure is via the **CALL** instruction. The following example defines the syntax for using the **CALL** instruction:

```
call            operand
Where:
operand         is a label, Reg16, or Mem16.
```

There are two basic types of calls: near and far. Near calls are calls to a procedure that resides in the same code segment as the section of the program that is doing the calling. To perform a near call, only a 16-bit offset is required. Before the 8088 microprocessor branches to the called procedure, it pushes the 16-bit address of the next instruction to be executed onto the stack. The following example shows a variety of near procedure calls:

```
        .
        .
call    addint              ;Call a procedure called
                            ; addint
call    near addint         ;Explicitly call addint as
                            ; a near call
call    bx                  ;Call the procedure whose
                            ; address is in BX
call    word ptr [bx]       ;Call the procedure whose
                            ; address is pointed to by
                            ; BX
        .
        .
```

A far call can be a call to a procedure that resides anywhere in the computer's memory. Therefore, it can either reside in the current code segment or any other code segment. Note that any procedure that is called as a far call must have been defined as **FAR** in its **PROC** statement. To perform a far call, a segment address and an offset address are required. Before the 8088 microprocessor branches to a called far procedure, it pushes the current value of the **CS** register and the address of the next instruction to be executed onto the stack. The following example shows a variety of far procedure calls:

```
        .
        .
        call    addint              ;Call a procedure named
                                    ; addint
        call    far addint          ;Explicitly call addint as
                                    ; a far call
        call    dword ptr [bx]      ;Call the procedure whose
                                    ; address is pointed to by
                                    ; BX
        .
        .
```

Returning from a Procedure

Returning from a called procedure is performed by a **RET** instruction. If a **NEAR** procedure was called, a **RET** instruction pops the first word off the stack into **IP**. If a **FAR** procedure was called, a **RET** instruction pops the first word off the stack into **IP** and then pops the next word on the stack into **CS**. A **RET** instruction determines whether its associated procedure is near or far by the type specification in the procedure's **PROC** directive. A **RET** statement can also optionally remove a specified number of bytes from the stack after it has removed the return address from the stack. As you will see in the next section, this optional feature of the **RET** instruction comes in handy for removing arguments that have been passed to the procedure via the stack. The following example defines the syntax for the **RET** instruction:

```
    ret         bytes
    Where:
    bytes                   is an optional immediate value that
                            specifies how many bytes are to be
                            removed from the stack after the return
                            address has been popped.
```

The following program fragment illustrates how an assembly language procedure adds two integer values in registers AX and **BX** and returns the result in **AX**:

```
            •
            •
            •
main proc
            •
      mov     ax,33    ;Put the first argument in AX
      mov     bx,44    ;Put the second argument in BX
      call    addint   ;Figure the total
            •
main endp
            •
            •
            •
addint      proc
      add     ax,bx    ;Figure the result
      ret              ;Return
addint      endp
            •
            •
```

Arguments

As you saw in the previous example, a procedure often requires one or more arguments to be passed to it in order to perform its assigned task. Procedure arguments can be passed using three fairly simple methods:

- in registers
- on the stack
- with pointers to the actual arguments either in registers or on the stack.

The previous example showed how arguments could be passed in registers. This is an easy and fast method for passing arguments. However, for more complex programs, passing arguments by registers is not always practical.

Arguments can be passed on the stack by putting them in a register and pushing them on the stack before the procedure is called. The following program fragment is a revised version of the **addint** procedure that now uses arguments on the stack instead of arguments in registers:

```
        .
        .
main    proc
        .
        mov    ax,33        ;Put the first argument in AX
        push   ax           ;Put it on the stack
        mov    ax,44        ;Put the second argument in AX
        push   ax           ;Put it on the stack
        call   addint       ;Figure the total
        .
main    endp
        .
        .
addint  proc   near
        push   bp           ;Save BP
        mov    bp,sp        ;Point BP to the bottom of the
                            ; stack
        mov    ax,[bp + 6]  ;AX = First argument
        add    ax,[bp + 4]  ;Add the second argument to AX
        pop    bp           ;Restore BP
        ret    4            ;Return and clean up the stack
addint  endp
        .
        .
```

As you can see from this example program, the two arguments are placed in **AX** and pushed on the stack before the procedure is called. Once execution has been passed to the procedure, the arguments are accessed through the **BP** register. To accomplish this, the **BP** register is first saved on the stack. Next, it is set to the current stack pointer location. Since **BP**'s default segment is **SS**, it can now be used to point to anything on the stack. The figure 11-1 illustrates what the stack would look like at this point:

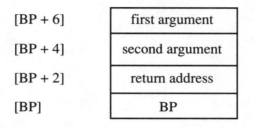

[BP + 6]	first argument
[BP + 4]	second argument
[BP + 2]	return address
[BP]	BP

Figure 11-1. The Stack Frame.

As the example shows, the procedure's arguments are on the stack in a stack frame and the first argument can be accessed through [BP + 6] and the second argument can be accessed through [BP + 4]. If this had been a call to a far procedure, [BP + 8] and [BP + 6] would have to be used because the return address would be a 32-bit value rather than the 16-bit value a near procedure uses. Note that the procedure restores BP before it returns the calling program. Furthermore, the **ret 4** instruction removes the arguments from the stack before program execution is actually returned. Although the **ret 4** is probably the fastest and easiest method for removing the arguments from the stack, they can also be removed by the calling program after execution has been returned. The following program fragment is a revised example of the **addint** program; it removes the arguments from the calling program:

```
          .
          .

main      proc
          .
          mov    ax,33          ;Put the first argument in AX
          push   ax             ;Put it on the stack
          mov    ax,44          ;Put the second argument in AX
          push   ax             ;Put it on the stack
          call   addint         ;Figure the total
          add    sp,4           ;Remove the arguments from the
                                ; stack

          .
main      endp
          .

          .
addint    proc   near
          push   bp             ;Save BP
          mov    bp,sp          ;Point BP to the bottom of the
                                ; stack
          mov    ax,[bp + 6]    ;AX = First argument
          add    ax,[bp + 4]    ;Add the second argument to AX
          pop    bp             ;Restore BP
          ret                   ;Return and clean up the stack
addint    endp
          .
          .
```

The following example of the addint program shows how it uses pointers on the stack to pass parameters to the procedure:

```
            •
            •
arg1    dw      33
arg2    dw      44
            •
            •
main    proc
            •
        mov     ax,offset arg1  ;AX = Pointer to 1st
                                ; argument
        push    ax              ;Put it on the stack
        mov     ax,offset arg2  ;AX = Pointer to 2nd
                                ; argument
        push    ax              ;Put it on the stack
        call    addint          ;Figure the total
            •
main    endp
            •
            •
addint  proc    near
        push    bp              ;Save BP
        mov     bp,sp           ;Point BP to the bottom of
                                ; the stack
        push    bx              ;Save BX
        mov     bx,[bp + 6]     ;BX = 1st argument pointer
        mov     ax,[bx]         ;AX = 1st argument
        mov     bx,[bp + 4]     ;BX = 2nd argument pointer
        add     ax,[bx]         ;Figure the result
        pop     bx              ;Restore BX
```

continued…

…from previous page

```
        pop     bp              ;Restore BP
        ret     4               ;Return and clean up the
                                ; stack

        addint  endp
        .
        .
```

Summary

In this chapter, you learned how you can use assembly language procedures like high-level language procedures and functions. You saw how they are called and how they return program execution to the calling program. Additionally, the chapter discussed the three major methods for passing arguments to an assembly language procedure.

Chapter 12

Ports

The 8088 microprocessor has a number of **ports** that enable it to communicate with input and output devices. These ports directly transfer data between either an accumulator or memory and a peripheral device. This chapter teaches you about the 8088 assembly language instructions that allow data transfer through ports.

IN Instruction

The **IN** (**in**put from port) instruction fetches either a byte or a word value from a specified port and places it in the accumulator. The number of bits in the value to be fetched is determined by whether **AL** or **AX** is being used for the accumulator. The following example defines the syntax for using the **IN** instruction:

```
in              accumulator,port
```

Where:

accumulator   is either AL or **AX**.

port   is the port number to fetch the byte or
                         word value from. The port number can be
                         either specified in register DX or an
                         Imm8. Since immediate values are lim-
                         ited to eight bits, register **DX** must be
                         used to specify a port number greater
                         than 255.

The following program fragment is an example of assembly language statements that use the **IN** instruction to fetch data from a port:

```
     .
     .
in     al,3          ;Fetch a byte from port 3 into AL
mov    dx,0f35h      ;DX = Port number
in     al,dx         ;Fetch a byte from DX's port
inc    dx            ;Bump the port number
int    ax,dx         ;Fetch a word from DX's port
     .
     .
```

OUT Instruction

The **OUT** (output to port) instruction sends either a byte or a word value in the accumulator to a specified port. The number of bits in the value to send is determined by whether **AL** or **AX** is being used for the accumulator. The following example defines the syntax for using the **OUT** instruction:

out   `port,accumulator`

Where:

`port`   is the port number to send the byte or word value to. The port number can either be specified in register DX or an Imm8. Since immediate values are limited to eight bits, register **DX** must be used to specify a port number greater than 255.

`accumulator`   is either **AL** or **AX**.

The following program fragment is an example of assembly language statements that use the **OUT** instruction:

```
        .
        .
    out     5,ax            ;Send the value in AX to
                            ; port 5
    mov     dx,03ffh        ;DX = Port number
    out     dx,ax           ;Send a word out DX's port
    dec     dx              ;Decrement the port number
    out     dx,al           ;Send a byte out DX's port
        .
        .
```

INS, INSB, and INSW Instructions

The **INS** (**in**put string from port), **INSB** (**in**put **b**yte string from port), and **INSW** (**in**put **w**ord string from port) instructions fetch either a byte or word value from a port and store it in a string location. The string is pointed to by **ES:DI** and the value to be stored is fetched from the port specified by **DX**. After each instruction is executed, **DI** is either incremented or decremented according to the value of the **direction** flag. If the **direction** flag is cleared by the **CLD** instruction, register **DI** is incremented once for byte strings or incremented twice for word strings. Conversely, **DI** is decremented once for byte strings or decremented twice for word strings when the **direction** flag has been set by the **STD** instruction. The following example defines the syntax for the **INS** instruction:

```
ins             destination
Where:
destination          is the location of the string.

Note:
In addition to indicating the address of the string, the
destination operand indicates whether a byte or a word is
to be fetched from the specified port.
```

The following example defines the syntax for the **INSB** instruction:

```
insb
```

The following example defines the syntax for the **INSW** instruction:

```
insw
```

The following program fragment is an example of assembly language statements that use the **INS** instruction:

```
            .
            .
_DATA    segment   word public 'DATA'
buffer   db        10 dup (?)
_DATA    ends
            .
            .
_TEXT    segment   word public 'CODE'
         assume    cs:_TEXT,ds:_DATA
            .
            .
         mov       ax,_DATA        ;Set
         mov       es,ax           ; ES
         lea       di,buffer       ;ES:DI = Buffer pointer
         mov       dx,0dfeh        ;DX = Port number
         mov       cx,10           ;CX = Loop counter
         cld                       ;Flag increment
ll:      ins       buffer          ;Get a byte from the port
                                   ; and store it
         loop      ll              ;Loop till done
            .
            .
```

12 Ports

The previous program fragment uses the **INS** instruction to fetch a 10-byte string from a port and store it in an appropriate buffer area. The following program fragment accomplishes the same task, but uses the **INSB** instruction instead of the **INS** instruction:

```
             .
             .

_DATA     segment   word public 'DATA'
buffer    db        10 dup (?)
_DATA     ends
             .
             .

_TEXT     segment   word public 'CODE'
          assume    cs:_TEXT,ds:_DATA
             .
             .
          mov       ax,_DATA          ;Set
          mov       es,ax             ; ES
          lea       di,buffer         ;ES:DI = Buffer pointer
          mov       dx,0dfeh          ;DX = Port number
          mov       cx,10             ;CX = Loop counter
          cld                         ;Flag increment
l1:       insb                        ;Get a byte from the port
                                      ; and store it
          loop      l1                ;Loop till done
             .
             .
```

The following program fragment is similar to the previous two examples except that it fetches a string of five words from a specified port:

```
                   •
                   •
        _DATA   segment   word public 'DATA'
        buffer  dw        5 dup (?)
        _DATA   ends
                   •
                   •
        _TEXT   segment   word public 'CODE'
                assume    cs:_TEXT,ds:_DATA
                   •
                   •
                mov       ax,_DATA        ;Set
                mov       es,ax           ; ES
                lea       di,buffer       ;ES:DI = Buffer pointer
                mov       dx,0dfeh        ;DX = Port number
                mov       cx,5            ;CX = Loop counter
                cld                       ;Flag increment
        l1:     insw                      ;Get a word from the port
                                          ; and store it
                loop      l1              ;Loop till done
                   •
                   •
```

The REP Prefix

Like many of the other 8088 string instructions, the **REP** prefix can simplify using the INS family of instructions. The following program fragment is similar to the **INSW** example except that this version uses the **REP** prefix instead of a **LOOP** instruction:

```
        .
        .

_DATA   segment   word public 'DATA'
buffer  dw        5 dup (?)
_DATA   ends

        .
        .

_TEXT   segment   word public 'CODE'
        assume    cs:_TEXT,ds:_DATA

        .
        .

        mov       ax,_DATA          ;Set
        mov       es,ax             ;ES
        lea       di,buffer         ;ES:DI = Buffer pointer
        mov       dx,0dfeh          ;DX = Port number
        mov       cx,5              ;CX = Loop counter
        cld                         ;Flag increment
        rep       insw              ;Get the string from the
                                    ; port

        .
        .
```

OUTS, OUTSB, and OUTSW Instructions

The **OUTS** (output string to port), **OUTSB** (output byte string to port), and **OUTSW** (**out**put word string to port) instructions send either a byte or word value from a string to a specified port. The string is pointed to by **DS:SI** and the port number to send the value to is specified by **DX**. After each instruction is executed, **SI** is either incremented or decremented according to the value of the **direction** flag. If the **direction** flag has been cleared by the **CLD** instruction, register **SI** is incremented once for byte strings or twice for word strings. Conversely, **SI** is decremented once for byte strings or decremented twice for word strings when the **direction** flag has been set by the **STD** instruction. The following example defines the syntax for the **OUTS** instruction:

```
outs            source
Where:
source               is the string's location.
```

Note:

```
In addition to indicating the string's storage address, the
source operand indicates whether a byte or a word is to be
sent to the specified port.
```

The following example defines the syntax for the **OUTSB** instruction:

```
outsb
```

The following example defines the syntax for the **OUTSW** instruction:

```
outsw
```

12 Ports

The following program fragment is an example of assembly language statements that use the **OUTS** instruction:

```
                •
                •
    _DATA    segment   word public 'DATA'
    string   db        10 dup (?)
    _DATA    ends
                •
                •
    _TEXT    segment   word public 'CODE'
             assume    cs:_TEXT,ds:_DATA
                •
                •
             mov       ax,_DATA          ;Set
             mov       ds,ax             ; DS
             lea       si,string         ;DS:SI = String pointer
             mov       dx,0feh           ;DX = Port number
             mov       cx,10             ;CX = Loop count
             cld                         ;Flag increment
    ll:      outs      string            ;Send a byte to the port
             loop      ll                ;Loop till done
                •
                •
```

The previous program fragment uses the **OUTS** instruction to send a 10-byte string out of a specified port. The following program accomplishes the same task, but uses the **OUTSB** instruction instead of the **OUTS** instruction:

```
            .
            .
_DATA       segment    word public 'DATA'
string      db         10 dup (?)
_DATA       ends
            .
            .

_TEXT       segment    word public 'CODE'
            assume     cs:_TEXT,ds:_DATA
            .
            .

            mov        ax,_DATA            ;Set
            mov        ds,ax               ; DS
            lea        si,string           ;DS:SI = String pointer
            mov        dx,0feh             ;DX = Port number
            mov        cx,10               ;CX = Loop count
            cld                            ;Flag increment
l1:         outsb                          ;Send a byte to the port
            loop       l1                  ;Loop till done
            .
            .
```

12 Ports

The following program fragment is similar to the previous two examples except that it sends a string of five words out of a specified port:

```
            .
            .

_DATA       segment    word public 'DATA'
string      db         5 dup (?)
_DATA       ends
            .
            .

_TEXT       segment    word public 'CODE'
            assume     cs:_TEXT,ds:_DATA
            .
            .
            mov        ax,_DATA          ;Set
            mov        ds,ax             ; DS
            lea        si,string         ;DS:SI = String pointer
            mov        dx,0feh           ;DX = Port number
            mov        cx,5              ;CX = Loop count
            cld                          ;Flag increment
ll:         outsw                        ;Send a word to the port
            loop       ll                ;Loop till done
            .
            .
```

The REP Prefix

Like the **INS** family of instructions and many of the other 8088 string instructions, the **REP** prefix can simplify using the **OUTS** family of instructions. The following program fragment is similar to the **OUTSW** example except that this version uses the **REP** prefix instead of a **LOOP** instruction:

```
        .
        .
_DATA   segment   word public 'DATA'
string  db        5 dup (?)
_DATA   ends
        .
        .
_TEXT   segment   word public 'CODE'
        assume    cs:_TEXT,ds:_DATA
        .
        .
        mov       ax,_DATA        ;Set
        mov       ds,ax           ; DS
        lea       si,string       ;DS:SI = String pointer
        mov       dx,0feh         ;DX = Port number
        mov       cx,5            ;CX = Loop count
        cld                       ;Flag increment
        rep       outsw           ;Send a word to the port
        .
        .
```

Summary

This chapter taught you how the 8088 microprocessor uses ports to transfer data between the computer and peripheral devices. Furthermore, this chapter introduced you to the wide range of instructions the 8088 microprocessor offers for performing the actual data transfers through ports. Additionally, you learned that these instructions allow single bytes, words, and whole strings to be transferred via the 8088's ports.

Chapter 13

Interrupts

O ften a hardware device requires the immediate attention of the CPU to correctly process a certain event. The hardware device generates a hardware interrupt to get the attention of the 8088 microprocessor and to halt the program that is running. This chapter teaches you

- how the 8088 microprocessor handles interrupts
- how to use the 8088 assembly language instructions that process interrupts.

8088 Interrupts

An interrupt causes the 8088 to halt the currently executed program. Once the program is halted, the 8088 saves a number of key registers on the stack and calls a predefined interrupt handler. Upon return from the interrupt handler, the 8088 pops the registers off the stack and resumes execution of the program from where it was interrupted. If the interrupt enable flag is set, the 8088 microprocessor honors the interrupt by calling the interrupt's associated interrupt handler. The address of the interrupt handler is determined by looking it up in the interrupt description table. The 8088's interrupt description table is located in memory at 0000:0000H.

Each interrupt handler requires a 32-bit far pointer to the its corresponding address in the computer's memory. The legitimate range of 8088 interrupts is 0 to 255. Thus, the interrupt description table is 1024 bytes (256 interrupts * 4 bytes) long.

Before the CPU actually jumps to the address of the interrupt handler, it first pushes the flags, the code segment (**CS**), and the instruction pointer (**IP**) onto the stack. Additionally, the 8088 clears both the **trap** and **interrupt** enable flags. After jumping to the interrupt handler, the interrupt routine is executed until an **IRET** instruction is encountered. The **IRET** causes the 8088 to pop the instruction pointer, the code segment, and the flags off the stack.

In addition to hardware interrupts, an interrupt can be generated by an assembly language instruction: **INT**. The **INT** (**int**errupt) instruction simply executes the interrupt handler for a specified interrupt number. On a PC, software interrupts make calls to functions, such as, ROM BIOS routines or DOS routines. For example, interrupt 21H performs the majority of DOS routines. The following example defines the syntax for the **INT** instruction:

```
int         number
Where:
number              is the number of the interrupt to be
                    called. It must be in the range of 0 to
                    255.
```

The following program fragment is an example of assembly language statements that use the **INT** instruction:

```
        .
        .
mov     dx,offset string        ;DX = String pointer
mov     ah,09h                  ;AH = DOS function call
int     21h                     ;Display the string
        .
        .
```

The 8088 has an **INTO** (**int**errupt on **o**verflow) instruction to call an interrupt handler. It is similar to the **INT** instruction; however, the **INTO** instruction specifically calls interrupt 04h if the overflow flag has been set. If the overflow flag has not been set, the **INTO** instruction is ignored. The following example defines the syntax for **INTO** instruction:

```
    into
```

The following program fragment is an example of assembly language statements that use the **INTO** instruction:

```
        .
        .
add     ax,0fff3h               ;Add 0FFF3H to AX
into                            ;Generate an interrupt if
                                ; the result overflowed
        .
        .
```

Interrupt Handlers

An interrupt handler is defined much like any other assembly language procedure. However, an interrupt routine must be defined as a **FAR** procedure and it is terminated with an **IRET** instruction instead of a **RET** instruction. The following example illustrates the format for constructing an interrupt handler:

```
name     proc  far
           .
           .
           .
         iret
name     endp
```

Where:

```
name                    is the name of the interrupt procedure.
```

The following program fragment illustrates how an assembly language interrupt handler is implemented:

```
           .
           .
_DATA    segment   word public 'DATA'
string   db        "Overflow error", 13, 10, "$"
old4     dd        ?
_DATA    ends
           .
           .
_TEXT    segment   word public 'CODE'
         assume    cs:_TEXT,ds:_DATA
main     proc
         mov       ax,_DATA       ;Set
         mov       ds,ax          ; DS
```

continued…

...from previous page

```
        mov    ah,35h                ;AH = Get int vector
                                     ; function code
        mov    al,4                  ;AL = Interrupt number
        int    21h                   ;Get the current INT 4
                                     ; address
        mov    word ptr old4[2],es   ;Save the segment address
        mov    word ptr old4[0],bx   ;Save the offset
        push   ds                    ;Save DS
        mov    ax,cs                 ;Set DS with
        mov    ds,ax                 ; the segment address
        mov    dx,offset overflow    ;DX = Offset address
        mov    ah,25h                ;AH = Set int vector
                                     ; function code
        mov    al,4                  ;AL = Interrupt number
        int    21h                   ;Set the new interrupt
                                     ; address
        .
        .
        add    ax,0fff3h             ;Add 0FFF3H to AX
        into                         ;Call INT 4 if overflow
        .
        .
        lds    dx,old4               ;DS:DX = Old INT 4 ad-
                                     ; dress
        mov    ah,25h                ;AH = Set int vector
                                     ; function code
        mov    al,4                  ;AL = Interrupt number
        int    21h                   ;Restore the old inter-
                                     ; rupt
        mov    ah,4ch                ;AH = DOS exit program
                                     ; function code
```

continued...

...from previous page

```
            mov  al,0              ;AL = Return code
int         21h                    ;Return to DOS
main        endp
            .
            .
overflow    proc far
            push ax                ;Save the
            push dx                ; registers
            sti                    ;Enable the interrupts
            mov  ah,9              ;AH = Display string
                                   ; function code
            mov  dx,offset string  ;DX = Error message
                                   ; address
            int 21h                ;Display the error mes-
                                   ; sage
            pop  dx                ;Restore
            pop  ax                ; the registers
            iret                   ;Return
overflow    endp
            .
            .
            end  main
```

Enabling and Disabling Interrupts

The final piece to the interrupt puzzle involves the instructions for enabling and disabling the interrupts. The **CLI** (**c**lear interrupt flag) instruction disables the interrupts and the **STI** (**s**et interrupt flag) instruction enables the interrupts. Note that when the interrupts are disabled by a **CLI** instruction, any interrupts that occur take place as soon as an **STI** instruction is executed. However, multiple interrupts by the same device are lost. This can cause problems with time-related interrupts if the interrupts are disabled for an extended period of time. The following example defines the syntax for the **CLI** instruction:

```
cli
```

The following example defines the syntax for the **STI** instruction:

```
sti
```

Summary

In this chapter, you learned how interrupts can temporarily interrupt a program's execution to execute a related interrupt handler. Furthermore, you learned how a software call to an interrupt handler is made and how an interrupt routine is actually implemented. Finally, the chapter presented the instructions for enabling and disabling interrupts.

Chapter 14

Conditional Assembly

The 8088 assembly language has conditional assembler directives like high-level languages have conditional compiler directives. These conditional assembler directives enable you to create one source code file for multiple versions of the same program. This chapter teaches you how to use these 8088 conditional assembler directives:

- IF...ENDIF
- IF...ELSE...ENDIF
- IFDEF...ENDIF
- IFNDEF...ENDIF.

The IF...ENDIF Conditional Directives

The simplest form of an 8088 conditional assembler directive is the **IF...ENDIF** combination of directives. The following example shows the format for using the **IF...ENDIF** directives. The example also shows that the assembly language statements between the **IF** and **ENDIF** directives are assembled only if the specified expression returns a true value. If the expression returns a false value, none of the **IF...ENDIF** statements are assembled.

```
if          expression

statement

   .

   .

statement
endif
```

Where:

```
expression          is an expression that returns either a
                    true or false value.

statement           is an assembly language statement.
```

The following program fragment illustrates how to use the **IF...ENDIF** conditional directives:

```
   .
   .
if      version eq 2
mov     ax,2                      ;This statement will be
                                  ; assembled if
                                  ; version is equal to 2

endif
   .
   .
```

246

IF...ELSE...ENDIF Conditional Directives

In addition to permitting simple **IF...ENDIF** conditional directives, 8088 assembly language also enables you to create a conditional directive that has an **ELSE** clause. Simply put, the assembler assembles any statements between the **IF** and **ELSE** directives if the **IF**'s expression returns true. Otherwise, the assembler assembles any statements between the **ELSE** and **ENDIF** directives for an **IF** expression that returns a false value. The following example illustrates the format for using the **IF...ELSE...ENDIF** directives:

```
if          expression
statement
.
.
statement
else
statement
.
.
statement
endif
```

Where:

expression   is an expression that returns either a
                    true or false value.

statement   is an assembly language statement.

The following program fragment illustrates how you use the **IF...ELSE...ENDIF** conditional directives in an assembly language program:

```
      .
      .
if    version eq 2
mov   ax,2                    ;This statement will be
                              ; assembled if
                              ; version is equal to 2
else
mov   ax,3                    ;This statement will be
                              ; assembled if
                              ; version isn't equal to 2
endif
      .
      .
```

IFDEF...ENDIF Conditional Directives

The **IFDEF...ENDIF** conditional directives assemble a group of assembly language statements only if a specified label, variable, or symbol has been defined. If the specified name has been defined, all of the statements between the **IFDEF** and **ENDIF** directives are assembled. Note that an **ELSE** clause can be combined with the **IFDEF**

and **ENDIF** directives in the same manner it is combined with the **IF...ENDIF** directives.
The following example illustrates the format for using the **IFDEF...ENDIF** directives:

```
        ifdef       name
        statement
        .
        .
        statement
        endif
```

Where:

name   is a previously defined label, vari-
                    able, or symbol.

statement   is an assembly language statement.

The following program fragment illustrates how you use the **IFDEF...ENDIF** conditional directives in an assembly language program:

```
            .
            .
            ifdef    MSC
_addint     proc     far
            endif
            .
            .
            ifdef    MSC
_addint     endp
            endif
            .
            .
```

IFNDEF...ENDIF Conditional Directives

The **IFNDEF...ENDIF** conditional directives assemble a group of assembly language statements only if a specified label, variable, or symbol has not been defined. If the specified name has not been defined, all of the statements between the **IFNDEF** and **ENDIF** directives are assembled. Note that an **ELSE** clause can be combined with the **IFNDEF** and **ENDIF** directives in the same manner it is combined with the **IF...ENDIF** and **IFDEF...ENDIF** directives. The following example illustrates the format for using the **IFNDEF...ENDIF** directives:

```
ifndef          name
statement
.

.
statement
endif
```
Where:

name   is a label, variable, or symbol that
                        hasn't been defined.

statement   is an assembly language statement.

The following program fragment illustrates how you use the **IFNDEF...ENDIF** conditional directives in an assembly language program:

```
            •
            •
            •
            ifndef   MSC
addint      proc     far
            endif
            •
            •
            ifndef   MSC
addint      endp
            endif
            •
            •
```

Summary

In this chapter, you learned how you can use conditional assembly directives to control how a program is assembled. Although these conditional assembly directives are fairly simple to use, you can use them to create a single source code file that generates multiple versions of the same program.

Chapter 15

Equates and Macros

A lthough procedures work well in medium to large sections of code, the overhead of calling and returning from small procedures can be significant. Fortunately, you can use equates and macros to provide a more efficient method for handling small sections of code that are repeated throughout a program. This chapter teaches you about

- nonredefinable numeric equates
- redefinable numeric equates
- string equates
- macros
- local labels
- repeat blocks
- exits from macros
- macro operators.

Nonredefinable Numeric Equates

The first type of an assembly language equate you need to be acquainted with is the **nonredefinable numeric equate**. Nonredefinable numeric equates allow a numeric constant to be assigned to a symbol name. Once assigned a numeric value, a symbolic name is replaced during assembly with its corresponding value. As its name implies, a nonredefinable numeric equate cannot be assigned a new value once it has been assigned. The following example illustrates how you use the **EQU** directive to define a nonredefinable numeric equate:

```
name            equ    expression
```
Where:
```
name                   is the name of a symbol.
expression             is a valid numeric expression.
```

The following program fragment is an example of assembly language statements that use the **EQU** directive to define nonredefinable equates:

```
        .
        .
string  db      '123456789'
strlen  equ     9
        .
        .
        mov     bx,offset string    ;BX = String pointer
        mov     cx,strlen           ;CX = String length
        call    disp_string         ;Display the string
        .
        .
```

Redefinable Numeric Equates

In addition to providing nonredefinable numeric equates, the 8088 assembly language enables you to define **redefinable numeric equates**. Like their nonredefinable counterparts, redefinable numeric equates assign a numeric constant to a symbol name. However, a redefinable numeric equate can be assigned a new value in another part of the program. Once assigned a numeric value, a symbol name is replaced during assembly with its corresponding value. The following example illustrates how the = directive defines a redefinable numeric equate:

```
name            =       expression
Where:
name                    is the name of a symbol.
expression              is a valid numeric expression.
```

The following program fragment is an example of assembly language statements that use the = directive to define a redefinable equate:

```
        .
        .
row     =       1
column  =       1
        .
        .
        mov     al,row          ;AL = Row number
        mov     ah,column       ;AL = Column number
        .
        .
row     =       3
column  =       45
        mov     al,row          ;AL = Row number
        mov     ah,column       ;AL = Column number
        .
        .
```

String Equates

You can use 8088 assembly language string equates to assign a string constant to a symbolic name. String equates are sometimes referred to as text macros. Once assigned a string value, the symbolic name is replaced by its assigned value when the assembler encounters it. Like nonredefinable numeric values, string equates use the **EQU** directive. However, string equates are redefinable just like redefinable numeric equates. The following example illustrates how the **EQU** directive defines a string equate:

```
name              equ    <expression>
```
Where:
```
name                     is the name of a symbol.
expression               is a valid string expression.
```
Notes:
```
Although the < and > symbols are strictly optional, you
should always use them to prevent the assembler from con-
fusing the string constant with a previously defined nu-
meric constant.
```

The following program fragment is an example of assembly language statements that use the **EQU** directive to define a string equate:

```
        .
        .
row     equ    <[bp + 6]>
column  equ    <[bp + 8]>
        .
        .
        mov    ax,row            ;AX = Row value
        mov    bx,column         ;BX = Column value
        .
        .
```

Macros

Although equates are very useful programming tools, assembly language macros are more powerful for quickly implementing short sections of code that are repeated throughout a program. You create macros with the **MACRO** and **ENDM** directives. The following example illustrates the format for defining a macro with the **MACRO** and **ENDM** directives:

```
name        macro        parameter, parameter, etc.
            statements
            .
            .
            statements
            endm
```

Where:

```
name                is the name of the macro.
parameter           is a replaceable parameter.
statements          is a valid assembly language statement.
```

The following example shows a macro definition:

```
addints    macro    int1,int2
           mov      ax,int1
           add      ax,int2
           endm
```

The previous macro example simply places the first parameter in **AX** and adds the value of the second parameter to it. The following example defines the syntax for using a macro in an assembly language program:

```
name    argument,argument,etc.
```

Where:

name   is the name of a previously defined
                        macro.

argument   is one or more arguments to be used as
                        substitutes for the macro's parameters.

Notes:

If more arguments are passed than were defined in the macro definition, the extra arguments are ignored by the assembler. If fewer arguments are passed than were defined in the macro definition, null strings are substituted for parameters that do not have a corresponding argument.

The following macro call uses the previously defined **addints** macro definition:

```
addints     3,4
```

When the assembler encounters the previous macro call, it substitutes the following statements for the macro:

```
mov     ax,3
add     ax,4
```

Local Labels

Since many routines require labels to branch execution to a new path, it isbetter to use labels inside of a macro. However, you can use macros more than once in the same program, which can very easily result in a label redefinition error. Consequently, macros must have a mechanism that allows labels to be redefined. You can redefine a label inside of a macro using local labels. Once defined, the assembler replaces a local label with a unique name for each instance of the macro throughout the program. The following example defines the syntax for creating a local label with the **LOCAL** directive:

```
local name,name,name
```

Where:

name   is one of more local label names.

The following example shows an assembly language macro that defines local labels:

```
movstring    macro    src_seg,src_off,dest_seg,dest_off,len
             local    l1
             push     ax
             push     cx
             push     di
             push     si
             push     ds
             push     es
             mov      ax,src_seg
             mov      ds,ax
             mov      si,src_off
             mov      ax,dest_seg
             mov      es,ax
             mov      di,dest_off
             mov      cx,len
             cld
l1:          movsb
             loop     l1
             pop      es
             pop      ds
             pop      si
             pop      di
             pop      cx
             pop      ax
             endm
```

Repeat Blocks

The 8088 assembly language also supports a special form of macro called a repeat block. Unlike a normal assembly language macro, a repeat block must be defined each time it is used in a program. The three different forms of 8088 assembly language repeat blocks are defined with the **REPT, IRP**, and **IRPC** directives.

REPT Repeat Blocks

The **REPT** directive creates a repeat block that is repeated for a specified number of times. The following example illustrates the format for defining a **REPT** repeat block:

```
rept              expression
statement
.

.
statement
endm
```

Where:

expression   is a numeric expression that defines how many times the block or statements will be repeated by the assembler.

statement   is a valid assembly language statement.

The following program fragment is an example of an **REPT** repeat block:

```
          .

          .

n         =         0
          rept      10
          db        n
n         =         n + 1
          endm
          .

          .
```

The previous **REPT** repeat block instructs the assembler to create a series of 10 **DB** directives with values of 0 to 9. The following example illustrates the statements the assembler would create as a result:

```
                    .
                    .
n           =       0
            db      n
n           =       n + 1
            db      n
n           =       n + 1
            db      n
n           =       n + 1
            db      n
n           =       n + 1
            db      n
n           =       n + 1
            db      n
n           =       n + 1
            db      n
n           =       n + 1
            db      n
n           =       n + 1
            db      n
n           =       n + 1
            db      n
n           =       n + 1
                    .
                    .
```

IRP Repeat Blocks

The **IRP** directive creates a repeat block that is repeated once for each of the arguments specified in an angle brackets (<>) list. The following example illustrates the format for defining a **IRP** repeat block. As the example shows, an **IRP** repeat block requires a single parameter. This parameter is replaced in the repeat block's statements by the values specified in the argument list.

```
irp          parameter,<argument,argument>
statement
    .

    .
statement
endm
```

Where:

parameter   is the parameter to be replaced by the arguments.

argument   is one of more arguments that the assembler substitutes for the repeat block's parameter.

statement   is a valid assembly language statement.

The following program fragment is an example of an **IRP** repeat block:

```
    .

    .
irp     n,<0,1,2,3,4,5,6,7,8,9>
db      n
endm
    .

    .
```

As you can see, the previous repeat block performs a function similar to the previous **REPT** repeat block example. However, the way the assembler actually interprets the

IRP repeat block is a little different than how it interprets the **REPT** repeat block. The following statements illustrate how an assembler would interpret the previous **IRP** block:

```
        •
        •
        db      0
        db      1
        db      2
        db      3
        db      4
        db      5
        db      6
        db      7
        db      8
        db      9
        •
        •
```

IRPC Repeat Blocks

The **IRPC** directive creates a repeat block that is repeated once for each character in a string argument. The following example illustrates the format for defining an **IRPC** repeat block. As the example shows, an **IRPC** repeat block requires a single parameter just like an **IRP** repeat block. The **IRPC** parameter is replaced in the repeat block's statements by the characters specified in the string argument:

```
irpc        parameter,argument
statement
.
.
statement
endm
```

Where:

parameter	is the parameter to be replaced by the argument's characters.
argument	is a valid string.
statement	is a valid assembly language statement.

The following program fragment is an example of an **IRPC** repeat block:

```
.
.
irpc   n,0123456789
db     n
endm
.
.
```

The previous program's **IPRC** repeat block performs the same function as the **IRP** repeat block example before it. The following statements illustrate how an assembler would interpret the previous **IRPC** block:

```
        .
        .
        db      0
        db      1
        db      2
        db      3
        db      4
        db      5
        db      6
        db      7
        db      8
        db      9
        .
        .
```

Exiting from a Macro

Occasionally, circumstances dictate that a macro should be exited from prematurely. The 8088 assembly language provides the **EXITM** directive for making an early exit from a macro. Essentially, the **EXITM** directive instructs the assembler to perform no further assembly on the macro. The following example shows a macro that uses the **EXITM** directive to ensure that a repeat block does not repeat out of control:

```
makebytes       macro     n
cnt             =         0
                rept      n
                if        cnt gt 255
                exitm
                endif
                db        cnt
cnt             =         cnt + 1
                endm
                endm
```

The previous macro is also a good example of nested macros (a macro defined inside of another macro). Note that the **EXITM** directive in the previous repeat block only halts further assembly of the **REPT** repeat block and not the **makebytes** macro. Although in this case, **makebytes** is simply a shell for implementing the **REPT** repeat block. Consequently, the **EXITM** directive effectively halts assembly for both macros.

The & Operator

The **&** operator enables you to force parameter substitutions for ambiguous parameter references. By prefixing a macro parameter with the **&** operator, the assembler substitutes the parameter's corresponding argument no matter where it appears in the macro definition. Although the **&** operator may not seem necessary, it allows the assembler to make parameter substitutions when a parameter is either preceded or followed by other characters, or when the parameter is in a quoted string. The following example defines the syntax for using the **&** operator:

```
&parameter
```

Where:

```
parameter          is a previously defined parameter.
```

The following program fragment illustrates how you use the **&** operator in a macro definition and a macro call:

```
                  .
                  .
message   macro         n
msg&n     db            'This is message no. &n'
          endm
                  .
                  .
          message       2
                  .
                  .
```

Since the **&** operator forces parameter substitutions, the previous **message 2** macro call would be assembled as follows.

```
msg5  db    'This is message no. 5'
```

The <> Operator

The **<>** operator instructs the assembler to treat the enclosed text as a literal string. This operator is particularly handy for passing a string like **1,2,3,4** as a macro argument. When you enclose them with the **<>** operator as **<1,2,3,4>**, the assembler treats the argument as just one argument instead of four individual arguments. The following example defines the syntax for the **<>** operator:

```
<text>
```
Where:
```
text                is a literal string.
```

The following program fragment illustrates how you use the **<>** operator in a macro call to pass an ambiguous text string as a single argument.

```
            .
            .
message     macro           string
            db              string,0
            endm
            .
            .
            message         <1,2,3,4>
            .
            .
```

Since the **<>** operator forces the assembler to treat the argument as a single string, the previous **message <1,2,3,4>** macro call would be assembled as follows:

```
      db      1,2,3,4,0
```

The ! Operator

The **!** operator instructs the assembler to treat the next character as a literal character and not a symbol. The **!** operator is quite useful for clarifying how an ambiguous character is to be assembled. The following example defines the syntax for the **!** operator:

```
!character
```
Where:
```
character           is a literal text character.
```

The following program fragment illustrates how you use the ! operator in a macro call
to clarify how an ambiguous character is to be assembled:

```
              •
              •
message    macro        string
           db           '&string',0
           endm
              •
              •
           message      <76 !> 75>
              •
              •
```

Since the ! operator forces the assembler to treat a succeeding character as a literal
character, the previous **message <76 !> 75>** macro call would be assembled as follows:

```
    db    '76 > 75',0
```

The % Operator

The **%** operator tells the assembler to evaluate an argument as an expression and to
substitute the result for the corresponding parameter. The **%** operator enables a macro
call to pass the value of a symbol name instead of the symbol name itself. The following
example defines the syntax for the **%** operator:

```
%text
```

Where:

```
text              is the symbol to be evaluated.
```

The following program fragment illustrates how you use the **%** operator in a macro call to evaluate an argument as an expression instead of a symbol:

```
                    .
                    .
message     macro          name,exp
            db             '&name = &exp',0
            endm
                    .
                    .
msg         equ            <Hi>
                    .
                    .
            message        msg,%msg
                    .
                    .
```

Since the **%** operator forces the assembler to treat an argument as an expression, the previous **message msg,%msg** macro call would be assembled as follows:

```
            db      'msg = Hi',0
```

Macro Comments

Although you can use ; comments in a macro definition, the assembler, under most circumstances, includes them in every macro call. By using **;;** instead of **;**, you can put a comment in a macro definition and the comment will not be included in any of the macro's calls. The following example defines the syntax for using a macro comment:

```
;;text
```
Where:
```
text                is the text to be treated as a comment.
```

The following example shows a macro definition that uses macro comments:

```
movstring       macro   src_seg,src_off,dest_seg,dest_off,len
                local   ll
                push    ax              ;;Save
                push    cx              ;; the
                push    di              ;; registers
                push    si
                push    ds
                push    es
                mov     ax,src_seg      ;;Set
                mov     ds,ax           ;; DS
                mov     si,src_off      ;;DS:SI = Source
pointer
                mov     ax,dest_seg     ;;Set
                mov     es,ax           ;; ES
                mov     di,dest_off     ;;ES:DI = Destination
pointer
                mov     cx,len          ;;CX = Number of byte
to move
                cld                     ;;Flag increment
ll:             movsb                   ;;Move a byte
                loop    ll              ;;Loop till done
                pop     es              ;;Restore
                pop     ds              ;; the
                pop     si              ;; registers
                pop     di
                pop     cx
                pop     ax
                endm
```

Summary

In this chapter, you learned how equates and macros can greatly simplify implementing short assembly language routines that are repeated throughout a program. This chapter also introduced you to three special macro types that create repeating blocks of assembly language statements. Finally, this chapter presented a number of macro operators and explained how to create macro comments.

Chapter 16

Interfacing Assembly Language with C and C++

Y ou rarely see an application program today that is coded entirely in assembly language programming. Indeed, the language of choice among many pro- grammers is C and its offspring C++. Although modern C and C++ compil- ers can produce remarkably efficient code, there are still times when it is necessary to enhance an application program with an assembly language routine. This chapter teaches you how to incorporate assembly language routines with your higher-level C programs using

- function and variable names
- parameter passing
- returns to the calling program
- local variable space.

Function and Variable Names

Selecting a C (for the remainder of this chapter, any references to C can also apply to C++) function or variable name is a fairly straightforward task. For example, a C function that searches an integer array for the highest value and returns the result could be named **search_array**. It is logical to assume that the name **search_array** can also be used for a similar assembly language procedure's name. Although **search_array** works for a few C compilers, most C compilers do not recognize **search_array** as a legitimate function name.

The most commonly used naming convention requires all function and variable names to begin with an _ (underscore). A few C compilers use a naming convention that requires all function and variable names to end with an _ character. These underscores are added to the function and variable names when the C compiler is compiling the program. Therefore, depending upon the C compiler, an assembly language **search_array** procedure could be named **search_array**, **_search_array**, or even **search_array_**. Although the variety of naming conventions can seem unwieldy, names for an assembly language routine that are used with more than one type of C compiler can be effectively handled with conditional assembly directives.

In addition to adhering to the naming convention of a C compiler, an assembly language function or variable name must be made global before a C program can either call the function or reference the variable. Therefore, all global assembly language function and variable names are declared public. By using a **public** assembly language directive, the linker can correctly link the assembly language procedures and variables to any C functions that use them. The following example defines the syntax for using the **public** directive to declare global the procedure and variable names.

```
        public      name,name,etc
Where:
name                is a procedure or variable name.
```

In addition to the C program needing access to an assembly language procedure or variable, the reverse can sometimes be true. Consequently, the assembly language prgram must be aware of any C function or variable names by declaring them as external names with the **EXTRN** directive. The following example defines the syntax for the **EXTRN** directive.

```
        extrn           name,name,etc.
Where:
name                    is the name of an external C function
                        or variable name.
```

Parameter Passing

The most common way a C compiler passes parameters to an assembly language procedure is to pass them on the stack in a stack frame. Note, however, that more and more C compilers are able to pass parameters to an assembly language procedure right in the CPU registers. Passing parameters in the CPU registers is the fastest method to accomplish parameter passing. However, passing parameters in stack frames is mostly a universal standard among compilers. For compatibility reasons, this should be used in all but extreme cases where speed is such an overriding concern that passing parameters in registers is more desirable than program portability.

Upon entry to an assembly language procedure the stack frame consists of a return address (two bytes for near calls or four bytes for far calls) followed by the first through the last parameters. The following example shows a stack frame for the **search_array** procedure.

Top of Stack	number	[BP + 10]
	array	[BP + 6]
	return address	[BP + 2]
Bottom of stack	BP	[BP]

*Figure 16-1. A **search_array** Stack Frame*

275

This stack frame assumes that **search_array** uses a C function prototype of **int far search_array(int far *array, int number);**. Since **search_array** is declared to be far, the C compiler puts a four-byte return address on the bottom of the stack. Additionally, the declaration of array as a **far** pointer means the C compiler puts a 32-bit far pointer on the stack instead of a 16-bit offset, which would be used if **array** was a **near** pointer. Although declaring the function as **far** and the array pointer as **far** is not strictly necessary for small memory model programs, most programmers use **far** pointers for all assembly language procedures. This prevents you from having to create a separate version of the assembly language routines for each of the memory models with which they may eventually be used.

By declaring everything as **far** in a C header file, the C compiler knows how to correctly call the assembly language procedure. Unfortunately, not all C compilers support mixed-memory model programming. Therefore, a separate version for each memory model may be necessary depending upon the C compiler you are using.

As soon as execution is passed from the C program to the assembly language procedure, the assembly language procedure must point register **BP** to the bottom of the stack to reference the passed parameters. The following program fragment illustrates how the proposed **search_array** procedure can accomplish this task.

```
array    equ     <[bp + 6]>
number   equ     <[bp + 10]>
         push    bp                       ;Set BP
         mov     bp,sp                    ;Point it to the stack
```

With BP pointing to the bottom of the stack frame, a **far** pointer to the array can be referenced using the offset **[bp + 6]**. Additionally, then number of elements to be searched can be referenced by an offset of **[bp + 10]**. Note how these offsets are given names with text equates. By naming the offsets, you greatly reduce the possibility of errors. After all, it's a lot easier to remember the name **array** than **[bp + 6]**. With the ability to access the parameters as **BP** offsets, you can continue coding the assembly language routines as follows.

```
        push    ds                      ;Save DS
        lds     si,array                ;DS:SI = Array pointer
        mov     cx,number               ;CX = Number of ele-
                                        ; ments
        mov     ax,0                    ;AX = Starting value
l1:     jcxz            l3              ;Jump if done
        cmp     ax,[si]                 ;Jump if AX
        jge     l2                      ; is >= this element
        mov     ax,[si]                 ;Put it in AX
l2:     inc     si                      ;Bump the
        inc     si                      ; pointer
        dec     cx                      ;Decrement the count
        jmp     l1                      ;Loop till done
l3:     pop     ds                      ;Restore
```

Returning to the Calling Program

Now that the assembly language procedure has performed its function, it must return to the calling C program with the result. With most C compilers, a value is returned to the calling program by placing the return value in a CPU register or a combination of CPU registers. Integer values are almost always returned in register **AX**. Since the result of the **search_array** procedure is already in register **AX**, no further steps are necessary to pass the value back to the calling C program. If, however, the result is in another register or a memory location, it has to be moved into register **AX** before execution is returned to the calling program.

In addition to preparing the return value, the assembly language procedure must clean up the stack before it returns to the calling C program. Since register **BP** was pushed onto the stack, it must be retrieved with a **pop bp** instruction. After retrieving register **BP** from the stack, the stack has been restored to its entry condition. Therefore, the assembly language procedure returns to the calling C program by executing a **ret** instruction. The C program removes the passed parameters from the stack before it continues on with its next task. The following example shows the remainder of the **search_array** procedure's code.

```
        pop     bp          ; the registers
        ret                 ;Return
```

The following example shows the complete listing for the **search_array** assembly language procedure.

```
;
; search.asm - Assembly language search integer array routine
;
SEARCH_TEXT     segment    para public 'CODE'
                assume     cs:SEARCH_TEXT
                public     _search_array
;
; Search array for highest element
;
_search_array   proc       far
array           equ        <[bp + 6]>
number          equ        <[bp + 10]>
                push       bp          ;Set BP
                mov        bp,sp       ;Point it to the stack
                push       ds          ;Save DS
                lds        si,array    ;DS:SI = Array pointer
                mov        cx,number   ;CX = Number of
                                       ; elements
```

continued...

...from previous page

```
                mov     ax,0        ;AX = Starting value
11:             jcxz    13          ;Jump if done
                cmp     ax,[si]     ;Jump if AX
                jge     12          ; is >= this element
                mov     ax,[si]     ;Put it in AX
12:             inc     si          ;Bump the
                inc     si          ; pointer
                dec     cx          ;Decrement the count
                jmp     11          ;Loop till done
13:             pop     ds          ;Restore
                pop     bp          ; the registers
                ret                 ;Return
_search_array   endp
SEARCH_TEXT     ends
                end
```

The following short C program demonstrates how the **search_array** assembly language procedure is used with an actual program. The chief thing to note about this program is how the function prototype is defined for the **search_array** procedure before it is called by the C program. By defining **search_array** in a function prototype, the C program can correctly call the assembly language procedure.

```
/*
    asmdemo.c - Assembly language interfacing demo
*/
#include <stdio.h>
#include <stdlib.h>
int far search_array(int far *array, int number);
int test_array[10] = { 2, 3, 55, 66, -2, 3, 4, 5, 9, 34 };
void main(void)
{
    int n;
    n = search_array(test_array, 10);
    printf("The highest element in test_array is %d.\n",n);
    exit(0);
}
```

Local Variable Space

Although the **search_array** procedure does not require stack space for local variables, many assembly language procedures do. Local variable space is allocated by subtracting the required number of bytes from the stack pointer. Suppose an assembly language procedure needs local variable space for two integers, **row** and **col**. The following assembly language code could allocate the necessary space.

```
        .
        .
    push    bp          ;Save BP
    mov     bp,sp       ;Point it to the stack
    sub     sp,4        ;Adjust stack for local variables
        .
        .
```

With the necessary local variable space allocated, the local variables can be referenced as negative offsets of register **BP**. Thus, row and col can be referenced by the offsets **[bp - 2]** and **[bp - 4]**. It really does not matter which location is selected for a variable; however, a variable's location must remain constant once it has been assigned.

Since the stack pointer is moved by the local variable space allocation, the assembly language function must deallocate the local variable space before attempting to restore register **BP**. Deallocation of the local variable space is accomplished by a **mov sp,bp** instruction. Recall that before the local variable space was allocated, register **BP** and **SP** were pointing to the same memory location. Therefore, loading register **SP** with the pointer in register **BP** effectively removes the local variable space from the stack. The following program fragment shows how an assembly language procedure deallocates its local variable space before returning to the calling program.

```
            .
            .
    mov     sp,bp       ;Restore the stack pointer
    pop     bp          ;Restore BP
    ret                 ;Return to the calling program
            .
            .
```

Assembly language procedures that do not require local variable space allocation should save the necessary registers just after the stack frame pointer has been set by the **mov bp,sp** instruction. Retrieving the saved registers must occur before register **BP** is restored during the assembly language procedure's exiting routine. Note that the **search_array** procedure properly saved and restored register **DS**. Assembly language procedures that do require local variable space allocation should not save the required registers until after the local variable space allocation has occurred. Accordingly, all of the saved registers must be retrieved before the assembly language procedure deallocates the local variable space. If the local variable space is deallocated first, the registers contents will be lost and erratic program execution is almost certain to result.

One last consideration must be taken into account by an assembly language procedure. Most C compilers require that certain CPU registers cannot be altered by an assembly language procedure. Therefore, any unalterable registers used in an assembly language procedure must be saved on the stack at the start of the assembly language procedure and retrieved from the stack before returning to the calling program.

Summary

In this chapter, you learned a number of important techniques for interfacing assembly language procedures with C programs. You saw how selecting the right name for an assembly language procedure can be very important. Additionally, this chapter covered such topics as parameter passing, returning values to the calling program, and local variable space. Finally, this chapter explained the importance of saving and restoring certain unalterable CPU registers.

Appendix

ASCII Code Table

ASCII CODES

Dec	Hex	Char	Dec	Hex	Char	Dec	Hex	Char	Dec	Hex	Char
0	00	NUL	32	20	[sp]	64	40	@	96	60	´
1	01	SOH	33	21	!	65	41	A	97	61	a
2	02	STX	34	22	"	66	42	B	98	62	b
3	03	ETX	35	23	#	67	43	C	99	63	c
4	04	EOT	36	24	$	68	44	D	100	64	d
5	05	ENQ	37	25	%	69	45	E	101	65	e
6	06	ACK	38	26	&	70	46	F	102	66	f
7	07	BEL	39	27	'	71	47	G	103	67	g
8	08	BS	40	28	(	72	48	H	104	68	h
9	09	HT	41	29	)	73	49	I	105	69	i
10	0A	LF	42	2A	*	74	4A	J	106	6A	j
11	0B	VT	43	2B	+	75	4B	K	107	6B	k
12	0C	FF	44	2C	,	76	4C	L	108	6C	l
13	0D	CR	45	2D	-	77	4D	M	109	6D	m
14	0E	SO	46	2E	.	78	4E	N	110	6E	n
15	0F	SI	47	2F	/	79	4F	O	111	6F	o
16	10	DLE	48	30	0	80	50	P	112	70	p
17	11	DC1	49	31	1	81	51	Q	113	71	q
18	12	DC2	50	32	2	82	52	R	114	72	r
19	13	DC3	51	33	3	83	53	S	115	73	s
20	14	DC4	52	34	4	84	54	T	116	74	t
21	15	NAK	53	35	5	85	55	U	117	75	u
22	16	SYN	54	36	6	86	56	V	118	76	v
23	17	ETB	55	37	7	87	57	W	119	77	w
24	18	CAN	56	38	8	88	58	X	120	78	x
25	19	EM	57	39	9	89	59	Y	121	79	y
26	1A	SUB	58	3A	:	90	5A	Z	122	7A	z
27	1B	ESC	59	3B	;	91	5B	[	123	7B	{
28	1C	FS	60	3C	<	92	5C	\	124	7C		
29	1D	GS	61	3D	=	93	5D	]	125	7D	}
30	1E	RS	62	3E	>	94	5E	^	126	7E	~
31	1F	US	63	3F	?	95	5F	_	127	7F	DEL

Index

Index

Index

MOVSB   170-174
MOVSW   170-174
MUL   91

N

NE   62
near call   215-216
NEG   84-85
negative numbers   39-41
nibbles   22
nonredefinable numeric equates   254
NOP   146
NOT (mnemonic)   101-102
NOT (operator)   56
numbers
  binary   36
  Boolean   41-42
  floating point   42
  hexadecimal   37-39
  negative   39-41
  positive   39-41
numeric equates
  nonredefinable   254
  redefinable   255

O

object module   16
OFFSET   66
operand   7-8
operation   7
operator precedence   72
operators   52-73, 79
OR (mnemonic)   103-104
OR (operator)   58
OUT   225
output devices   33
OUTS   231-235
OUTSB   231-235
OUTSW   231-235
overflow flag   32, 132, 135, 239

P

parameter passing   275-277
parity flag 31, 132, 136-137
POP   209-210
POPF   210-211
ports   223-235
positive numbers   39-41
precedence   72-73
PROC   214
procedure   214
program ports   7
program sample   9
PTR   71
PUBLIC   274
PUSH   209-210
PUSHF   210-211

Q

quadwords   25, 49

R

radix   51-52
RAM   32
RCL   108-109
RCR   109-110
record
  fields   205
  variables   201
records   199-205
redefinable numeric equates   255
register addressing   150-151
register indirect addressing   153-154
register set   27
registers   6, 27-32
REP   174, 183, 230, 235
REPE   188-189, 193
repeat blocks   260-265
repetition   163-167
REPNE   188-189, 193
REPNZ   188-189, 193